Marathon Runners

Marathon Runners

THOMAS BARRETT AND
ROBERT MORRISSEY, JR.

JULIAN MESSNER
NEW YORK

Manufactured in the United States of America.
Design by Irving Perkins Associates

Library of Congress Cataloging in Publication Data

Barrett, Thomas, 1931–
Marathon runners.

Includes index.
Summary: Presents profiles of five marathon
runners who have contributed to the increased
interest in this long distance event.
1. Runners (Sports)–Biography–Juvenile literature.
2. Marathon running–Juvenile literature.
[1. Runners (Sports)   2. Marathon running]
I. Morrissey, Robert.   II. Title.
GV1061.14.B37   796.4′26   [B][920] 81-11204
ISBN 0-671-34019-0   AACR2

To my grandmother Anna Morrissey

Thanks to DAVE PEARLMAN, the NEW
YORK ROAD RUNNERS CLUB, DICK ROTHCHILD
and ABE and SANDY SIMON.

Contents

INTRODUCTION

SET down in the following pages are profiles of a diverse group of marathon runners. We wrote this book with the hope that readers will be moved to pursue the adventure that lies just beyond their doorstep, adventure that will afford them another means of self-expression, reward them with good measures of health and joy, and fulfill them as do few other endeavors.

Thomas Barrett and Robert Morrissey, Jr.

Marathon Runners

Frank Shorter

THE MARATHON REVIVED

NO doubt about it, there is a revolution taking place in this country, a running revolution. By recent estimates, 30 million people have taken to the streets. Wherever you go, day or night, there they are, running along the side of the road, even in the worst kinds of weather. The poster picturing the start of the 1979 New York City Marathon on the Verrazano Narrows Bridge in all its immensity completely covered with runners leaves no doubt that a revolution is upon us.

It was set off by a most unlikely firebrand; a peaceful, ascetic person named Frank Shorter, who was a provocateur, nevertheless, to many of the 80 million Americans who watched him on ABC television running through the streets of Munich in the 1972 Olympic Marathon. He radicalized a great many of them; had such an effect upon them that as a result of having watched him run they changed their lives. The Munich marathon was a cultural happening, not unlike the Woodstock rock music festival in 1969, with the ripple-effect still being felt in American life as it moves in an ever-widening circle.

A number of things turned that marathon into a happening: Roone Arledge of ABC decided to give the marathon extensive coverage, and to bring in Erich Segal, a Yale classics professor and author of *Love Story*, for color commentary. Segal knows a lot about marathon running, having run many Boston marathons; he knows a lot about ancient Greece and the Olympic Games, and about Shorter who had been a student of his at Yale, and Segal is extremely articulate. The city of Munich helped by providing a backdrop of beauty in fall foliage, wide boulevards lined with monuments, splashing fountains, and splendid parks through which the marathon field wove.

The day was bright and hot, nearly 80 degrees, too hot and humid for running a marathon. The usual cool mountain breezes that descend from the surrounding Alps were absent; Shorter, however, had a lot to contribute. Television viewers saw him running, on and on, all alone, endlessly it seemed, across the ever-changing stage of Munich; moving with a grace that has not been matched in the world of distance running. A grace that comes from great efficiency of movement, like that of a cheetah racing across an African plain; no extraneous motion, just smooth fluidity, and buoyancy, always in the air floating, coming down only briefly with a light footfall and instant flick-off, and hands moving in staccato counterpoint. He looked as though he were flying. His gold Adidas, shaved thin to save weight, flashed sunspots on the screen, and the rhythmic rise and fall of his flowing dark hair was hypnotic. People had not seen anything like it before. This thin, Giacometti figure moving on and on amidst the luminous colors of fall. The beauty of it all was enchanting; an enchantment in sharp contrast to the siege of terror and killing of Israeli athletes a few days before.

Shorter was electrifying. He turned many people on to running. He aroused in them a primal instinct to run and got them to venture out of their houses and automobiles and into the world of nature; to see its beauty, to feel the sun and the rain; to hear the birds and experience intimately the change of seasons; and to become again the animal that each of us is. Those who ventured out to run, and there were many, discovered that the act of running put to use the equipment that evolution had given them, and by its use made them feel fulfilled, complete and whole and really alive; they were energized by it and left with feelings of satisfaction and joy. The word spread that running makes you feel good, and running became even more popular.

Shorter was race-prepared for the Olympic Marathon, pared of all excess; nobody had ever seen him thinner. Thin to the point of delicacy, he was greyhoundlike. At 125 pounds, his arms were like pipe-cleaners and his thighs only as thick as his calf muscles. You could count each of his ribs. At 5'10" he was called a "vertical hyphen," completely leaned out, with only 2.8 percent body fat, like a race car, with skin stretched tightly over thin tubing; a structure without much strength but enough to contain an engine, a large oxygen-gulping pump. Shorter's oxygen-uptake capacity of 7.1 liters is produced by a powerful heart that pumps like a jackhammer when it is pushed to 195 beats per minute, and when he is resting, at only 38 beats. The pencil-lead tracery of the vein system in his legs stands out against his muscles, as though it had been added on as an afterthought.

Before the start of the marathon in Munich, the runners were congregated in the grass infield of the track, looking each other over, assessing each other for weaknesses; in particular, they were looking at the thighs, looking for the carved-out, bowed quality that comes with fitness; fitness primarily of the heart, for a lean and sinewy thigh indicates a strong and conditioned heart, and the heart is the engine that pumps the fuel, the oxygen-laden blood to the muscles. Paul Dudley White, the eminent Boston cardiologist, always looked to the thighs first for an indication of the condition of the heart. Shorter studied in particular Ron Hill from England, Derek Clayton from Australia, and Akio Yusami from Japan. Hill was then number one in the world, having run a marathon in 2:09:28 only two years before in 1970. He was the only person to have broken 2:10, other than Derek Clayton. Clayton had run a 2:09:36 in 1967, and a 2:08:34 in 1969, which is the fastest marathon anyone has ever run over any course. He was the only marathoner to have broken the 2:09 barrier and the first to break 2:10. Yusami, a strong and powerful runner, had a 2:10:37 in 1970, and had finished behind Shorter by only 32 seconds, less than a year before at Fukuoka, Japan.

Hill was all aglimmer in his space suit of silver-mesh shirt and silver shorts. Silver would reflect the heat. Hill's shoes were also made of the same radiant, aerospace material, and had no tongues in them. The soles were too thin, Shorter thought, to protect the feet from blisters. Hill had shaved off his mustache and cut off most of his hair, which Shorter thought reflected his compulsiveness.

Derek Clayton was dressed in the colors of Australia, white track shorts and singlet with a yellow and light blue stripe and a kangaroo emblem. He is a big man, particularly for a marathoner, at 6'2" and 160 pounds. Shorter marked him, however, as not evidencing much strength. The stress of his 2:08 had left its mark upon Clayton. Years later, in *Runners World* magazine Clayton told of what had happened to him after finishing the 2:08: "What I don't think too many people can understand is what I went through for the next 48 hours [after the race he urinated clots of blood and vomited black mucus]. I have discussed this with the medical profession, asking them why this should be and I have not received a satisfactory answer. I only know one thing. After the 2:08, I was virtually finished. If anyone ever flattened themselves to run a race, I did on that particular day. I don't think anyone could realize just what it took out of my body."

While the sixty-nine runners stood on the track waiting for the officials to call the roll, some of them were looking up into the stadium for a certain tall, thin black man. He was there watching them intently from his wheelchair. He could not be down on the track with them because he could not move his legs. He had been badly injured in an automobile accident and left paralyzed from the waist down. His name was Abebe Bikila, from Ethiopia, a captain in Emperor Haile Selassie's Imperial Guard. Bikila had begun running in 1956 and only four years later was on his country's marathon team for the Olympic Games in Rome. The marathon was held at night because of the heat. Bikila ran as he had always run, barefooted, and he ran in a world and Olympic record time of 2:15:16. Four years later in 1964 he won the Olympic Marathon again, this time with shoes, in another world and Olympic record time 2:12:11. He won it in a decisive fashion, four minutes ahead of the next runner. Four years later the games were held in Mexico City. Bikila was running in the lead when fate struck him down for the first time. A stress fracture opened in the tibia bone of his left leg and he was forced to stop. A stress fracture is like the tiny cracks in a pane of glass and is caused by the stress of the foot striking over and over on unyielding pavement. His friend and running partner Mamo Wolde took over the lead from him and went on to win. A year later an automobile accident took from Bikila his beloved running and he died not many years later.

Emil Zatopek from Czechoslovakia was also watching from the stadium. He had been the marathon winner in the 1952 games. He won not only the marathon, but also the 5,000- and 10,000-meter races, the "triple crown" of distance running, and his wife Dana won the gold medal in the javelin throw. He is the only man ever to have won all three events. He was called the "Prague Express," and became known as the father of modern-day distance training. Although he did most of his training on a track, he was the first to do heavy mileage, upwards of 20 miles a day at a moderate pace, called LSO, long slow distance. The story is told of him that once when his wife wouldn't let him out of the house, he ran in place down in the cellar in a tub of laundry for nearly two hours. He also did most of his training runs in army combat boots. He said that when he raced in track shoes, it was like taking a day off. He once said: "If you want to win something, run 100 meters. If you want an experience, run a marathon."

After the officials had finished calling the roll of the marathoners, the gun cracked and the pack started around the track. Shorter crossed over to the inside lane and was soon in third place. The three Americans wore dark blue shorts and white racing singlets with "USA" in red and blue. They were easy to spot because they towered over the others; Jack Batcheler is 6'6", Kenny Moore over 6' and Shorter looked taller than his 5'10" because of his bolt-upright style. After two laps around the track, the runners went out through the tunnel under the stadium, each man moving as carefully as he could in the mob, fearing that any instant he would go down on the road in a tangle of feet, rolling, stepped on, with skinned knees. As the pace quickened the pack stretched out like a large glob of colorful taffy pulled by the leaders. Some of the runners were still talking in brief, cryptic exchanges, a diversion for the mind from the matters at hand.

Diverting the mind to something not connected with the act of running, something outside the body, is used for relaxation during the first third of the marathon and during the last third to give moments of relief from the pain. The thought occurring when the mind is diverted from thinking about running is called "disassociative thought." "Associative thought," on the other hand, deals with the act of running, the main component of which is the movement of one foot at a time by some 60 inches, more or less, ahead of the other, by a lift and drive of the leg from the knee to the butt, and thrust of the foot forward until it falls lightly on the heel and outside of the foot and rolls forward flicking off rapidly. These movements are instinctive to all of us, but in a race they must be governed to a pace that will enable the runner to endure for the distance.

Other components of the act of running on which the mind must be focused are where the foot will fall; the proper carriage and relaxation of the upper body, shoulder and hands; the breathing, often deep and pushing down the diaphragm; the condition of the muscles, particularly the hamstrings in the back of the thighs which are subject to cramping; and the pace, the rapidity of leg exchange and the length of the stride.

These associative thoughts directed to the act of running are like islands in the fast moving stream-of-conscious thought that floods across the mind in a never-ending flow from the eyes and ears. From the eyes come the views of the passing scene, the road, the footing, the holes and cracks in the pavement that can break an ankle in an instant, the crowds of people, their faces and clapping hands, the buildings, the officials' bus and photographers' truck that lead the way, the blue line painted on the road which marks the route, and so on and on. From the ears come the endless noise of shouts, cheering, clapping, church bells, dogs barking.

Other islands of thought that crop out in the stream-of-consciousness flowing through a runner's mind are thoughts drawn from the past triggered by connections between them and the things registered by the senses.

After Shorter and the rest of the marathon pack came out of the stadium tunnel they went over a bridge and soon found themselves backed up behind a flatbed truck carrying the photographers which had slowed to a snail's pace. Shorter tried to pass the truck on the right but just as he moved over, it moved over too, cutting him off and pushing him off the road. This cost him time, but gave him a shot of adrenaline which he needed because he was not feeling well even though the pace was slow. At the 3-mile mark the pace was only 5:10 a mile. The runners were holding back, fearful of the heat and high humidity.

In the early stage of the race each runner was trying to work out his rhythm, to make the stride exchange fluid, his footfalls light and the flick-off crisp, to make his breathing deep, and to make his upper body relaxed by dropping his hands and shoulders. He was trying also to get his mind used to the crowds and the noise by turning in on the spectators, by looking at and listening to their clapping and yelling, by touching hands with the kids that held them out, by drinking in the whole scene. Each runner was trying to conserve his power of concentration for use during the time when concentration would be in greatest demand, during the last 9 miles, and trying to be at peace with himself and his surroundings. The peace helps to preserve the adrenaline. He was also trying to position himself with his competitors and looking for someone to run with who had the same rhythm, because a runner can take a rhythm from another runner, as a piano player takes rhythm from a metronome.

As the string of runners left the main road and went into the ground of the Nymphenburg Castle, a large park, about 6 miles from the start of the race, ABC television took a break. Erich Segal pointed out to Jim McKay that from the Greeks' point of view, sport was as essential a part of life as any other cultural activity. No social status was accorded, however, to the hemero-dromoi, the all-day runner, who was a messenger not an athlete. Running was only his job. The longest race in the Greek Olympic Games was only about 3 miles. It was the dolichos, which was 24 stades in length, a stade being about 230 yards, the length of the course within the stadion at Athens.

In 490 B.C. the Greeks won a hard-fought battle on the plain outside the village of Marathon in Greece, 38 kilometers from Athens. The historian Herodotus, living at the time, and noted for his detailed and accurate reporting, made no mention of Pheidippides, the messenger who was supposed to have run from Marathon to Athens, announced, "Rejoice, victory is ours," and dropped dead. It was not until more than five hundred years later that any mention was made of Pheidippides and that was by Plutarch.

There is evidence that the Olympic Games took place in the fourteenth century B.C. However, it was not until 776 B.C. that there was any actual record of the games. Records have been found showing that Coroibos of Olis was the "Winner and Champion" that year of the stade race. The winner of an Olympic event was given a crown of wild olive leaves taken from the Altis, a sacred grove near the stadion in Athens, and he received a palm branch to hold when he was presented to the people. He became an honored citizen, exempt from taxation, and could live at public expense in the Prytraneum, a public hall in Athens for distinguished citizens and visitors. The Olympic Games were only a part of a large festival, which was religious in nature. The importance of the games was such that any Greek state warring with another would stop its fighting while the games took place. There were other Panhellenic Games besides those held in Athens. They were the Pythian Games, which were mainly musical competitions at which a crown of laurel leaves was given to the winners; the Nemian Games, held every two years at the Argive Festival, which had many kinds of athletic events, the winners of which received wreaths of wild cherry leaves; and the Isthmian Games held in Corinth, which included gymnastic, equestrian and musical competitions. In A.D. 393 Roman Emperor Theodosius decreed an end to the games. The Olympic flame was extinguished for 1,503 years.

The revival of the Olympic Games came through the efforts of one man, Baron Pierre de Coubertin of France, who conceived of the idea and was the sole director of the games from their revival in 1896 until 1924. He believed that peace would be furthered by the games, that peace would come to a world made up of better individuals, who, he thought, would be made better by the "stress and strain of fierce competition."

It was fitting that the first Olympic Games of the modern era were held in Athens, and that a Greek, Spiridon Loues was the winner of the first Olympic marathon, in the time of 2:58:50. The distance used then and in the next two games was about 24 miles or 38 kilometers, the distance from the village of Marathon to the city center of Athens. In 1908 the Olympics were held in London, England. The marathon distance there was stretched to 42.195 kilometers. This was done as the result of a birthday wish granted to the Princess of Wales, who later became Queen Mary. She wanted to watch the start of the race from her window in Windsor Castle and the finish at White City Stadium. The new distance became the standard used ever since that time.

At the 7-kilometer mark, Shorter and Kenny Moore came to the first water stop. Tables had been set up along the side of the road for the runners' plastic squeeze bottles. Each bottle had the same number as was on the racer's singlet. Shorter's number was 1014. Shorter and Moore, the day before, had taken Coca-Cola, shaken it up to get rid of the carbonation, and filled their squeeze bottles with it. Defused Coke was then the most popular runners' drink, because it contained water, sugar and some caffeine which helps to pick up the heart rate. Today the marathoners' bottles usually contain water and a mixed-in powder substance called ERG (electrolyte replacement and glucose). The drink contains trace elements of minerals that the runners sweat out, such as potassium, magnesium and salt, in the same proportions as exist in perspiration. It also contains glucose, a sugar.

When Shorter and Moore got to the tables, Shorter saw the runner ahead of him take his bottle. Instinctively, he took the next one. On a hot day fluid is absolutely essential for survival in a marathon. The bottle turned out to be Moore's, but Shorter could only apologize to him. He could not give it to him because this would cause Moore to be subject to disqualification, having been "aided." Shorter threw Moore's bottle down and sprinted after the runner who had taken his. When he caught him he grabbed the bottle out of his hand yelling, "That's mine."

At about seven miles Shorter began having problems with blisters. There was nothing much he could do except hope that they would not become too much and would eventually "numb up." Gaston Roelants from Belgium had taken the precaution of winding tape around his shoes to bind them to his feet in hopes of cutting down the friction and therefore the blistering. He was dressed all in white, a defense against the heat, as was Karl Lismont and Akio Yusami. Mamo Wolde, the defending Olympic champion, was dressed in green. With those runners in the lead pack was Jack Foster from New Zealand dressed all in black. He was thirty-nine years of age and had the year before run 80 laps on a track in 1:39, a new world record for 20 miles. Kenny Moore remarked on the appearance of Derek Clayton, who was running with Hill in the lead: "His arms were clawing high across his chest, his

Frank Shorter crossing the finish line in the 1972 Olympic Marathon in Munich. (HEINZ KLUETMEIER/*Sports Illustrated*)

head bobbing . . . his tongue rolling in and out of his mouth."
With Moore and Shorter was the third American, Jack Batcheler, the gentle giant.

Shorter likes to divide the marathon into thirds. The first
third he runs easily, the second third he runs hard, and the last
third he hangs on. The first third was over and he began to
move, to surge ahead. He broke away from the others first by
10 yards and then a little more and a little more. Nobody
came with him. It was too hot and they were afraid. But
Shorter runs well in the heat, better than in the cold. The heat
keeps him loose and the cold, particularly wet cold, tightens
him up.

Shorter comes out of the Nymphenburg Gardens and
back into the city streets, the camera and television trucks are
there again, the blue bus with the blinking red light leads him
on along the blue line marking the way. He is running all
alone. The bus is moving under an archway called the West
Gate. He can feel the hot sun and heat from the cobblestones
and asphalt through the thin soles of his Adidas. He has to
watch his footing on the cobblestones and the trolley tracks.
The large crowds, yelling and clapping, pick him up. His eyes
catch a flash of light from the store window . . . shopped there
last week . . . Neuhauser and Kaufinger Strasse . . . so expensive . . . Wolde heat trained. Yusami too. Why didn't they
come with me? . . . Too early? . . . It's all on the line. Why
not? Got to take risks. Watch cobblestones . . . holes . . . pick
up pace . . . clap clap clap . . . shouts, "Go U.S. Go U.S." . . .
Americans, med students at University of Munich . . . God,
how can they do it . . . German, impossible.

The blue electric bus with the blinking red light leads

him down Ludwigstrasse, past the Fish Fountain, his eyes catch the spitting and splashing, and his mind prints out a recollection, Fountains of Rome . . . Respigi. He hears the reverberations from the bells in the distance coming from Ludwigs-kirche . . . ding, dong, clang . . . big and heavy like the bells of St. John the Divine . . . clap clap clap . . . Germans clap politely . . . Americans yell and whistle . . . stone Bavarian lion . . . block letters on the street "20 kilometers." Time? I didn't hear it . . . what did they say? . . . one kilo to the aid station . . . push it, no dehydration . . . hamstrings o.k. no twinges . . . smooth . . . aid station . . . table there, break stride . . . where's my bottle number 1014 . . . got it . . . suck . . . warm, sweet. Man shouts, "30 seconds" . . . drop bottle. Is he right? Who is behind me? Wolde? . . . dangerous kick Wolde . . . push down diaphragm, blow it out . . . loosen up belly . . . knee lift lift drive drive . . . bus is running, cut over . . . stone lion . . . Konigsplatz . . . trolley tracks . . . watch footing . . . holes, shorten stride . . . feet burn . . . Oktoberfest 770,000 gallons of beer . . . eins, zwei, drei, . . . knee lift . . . lift drive . . . blue line . . . blue Wittlesbach blue, Munich blue electric blue . . . bus blinking light . . . shouts, press guys, "One minute" . . . My God, how can that be? . . . maintain, relax . . . easy easy . . . feel good . . . go now stride out out toe-point . . . cobblestone . . . feet sting burn . . . can live with . . . Wolde, he'll come. Why not? Not too hot for him. Not hot for Ethiopia. Press guy has one finger up—one minute. He must know. For sure. One minute. They can't make up . . . 10 seconds a mile for 6 miles . . . can't do it . . . don't go back to them . . . 4:50 pace too much for them . . . clap clap . . . restrained . . . so distant, so polite . . . you don't know about this business . . . blurrrr . . . bad patch, ease off, shorten stride, relax relax . . .

over, get over, bus moving over, cut corner, drop shoulders . . . faces faces smiles hands kids' hands. Ludwigstrasse . . . been here before. Ich bein ein Münchener . . . ein Berliner J.F.K. . . . clang, clang, time? Hour, what is it? . . . can't figure out . . . lift knees, lift up . . . watch tracks, intersection tracks, watch out . . . God, like cross-country . . . feet burn . . . cobblestones . . . granite blocks . . . Belgian blocks . . . clang, clang, clang . . . Ludwigskirche Towers . . . clang, clang . . . St. John . . . Glo-o-ri-a in ex-cel-sis De-o . . .

His eyes catch the large triumphal arch at the north end of Ludwigstrasse that resembles the Arch of Triumph in Paris. The arch is called Siegestor. The south side of the arch bears the inscription "Dedicated to Victory, Destroyed by War, Praying for Peace." The north side of it remains unrepaired from World War II, which left it pockmarked with bullet and shrapnel holes. He passes through one of its portals . . . smooth out roughness . . . be efficient . . . smooth German efficiency . . . born here, October 31, 1947 . . . Rommel tough, efficient . . . Hill shot? Too hot? . . . Silver Hill. Clayton? Too hot for him . . . he's too big . . . 2:08 finished him . . hang on, hold on to pace . . . sweating still, not dehydrated . . . One of them will get it together . . . somebody . . . Pace? 4:55? Too slow. No . . . Light footfall, quick crisp . . . blitz . . . blitzkrieg . . . tough tough running machine . . . Hold on to pace . . . Are they right? A minute? 400 yards? Not enough. Too slow . . . can catch me. Look back . . . can't see runners . . . bicycles . . . A runner? Bicycles with a runner? Blurr blurr . . . God I can't see a thing . . . bus going around corner. How far? Aid station coming . . . grab bottle number 1014. Go go. Squeeze, suck it out, throw it, get rid of it. Stride . . . move move. All alone, can't believe. Don't die. Clap clap bus blue line watch tracks silver tracks blue line silver tracks asphalt patch blocks steel tracks tracks . . . All of them tied up? Couldn't all be. Look back . . . can't see . . . look again . . . blurr blurr. Where is that press truck? Cobblestones . . . feet numb . . . can't feel blisters, hamstrings o.k., good shape . . . sweating good . . . drive drive, lift, pick up. Clap clap . . . fade . . . Man shouts something. What did he say? . . . Was it a name he yelled? Is someone coming? Look again. Look . . . nothing. Must have at least 200 or 300 yards. Pace pace pace . . . smooth smooth, feel rhythm. Buses turning off, going right. Over over, cut off corner, over . . . drop shoulder . . . watch out . . . tracks . . . tracks silver pewter tracks . . . There is entrance to English Garden . . . catching up to bus . . . people faces faces hands clap clap hands clap clap . . . clapping fades . . . on garden's foot path . . . rough path, move move, 9 miles left, don't let down . . . soft path . . . dusty . . .

As Shorter went into the English Garden, a large park at the northern end of Ludwigstrasse, ABC's Jim McKay and Erich Segal described some of the early Olympic marathons and showed film clips of the 1904 and 1908 marathons. In 1904, the summer games were held in St. Louis, Missouri. In the marathon, Fred Lorz of the United States was the leader until the halfway point when he dropped out. The heat and the pace had forced him to a halt. After being revived by water and rest, he got into one of the cars that was following the field. Eventually, the car passed all of the runners and, as luck would have it, broke down a few miles from the stadium. Lorz, having come back to life, ran the rest of the way and at the finish line he was greeted as the winner. Just before the award ceremonies, however, the officials found out what had happened and Lorz was disqualified. The consequence of his not having told the officials about his ride was his being banned for life from amateur competition. Despite the ban he ran and won the Boston Marathon the next year, 1905, in the time of 2:38.

In the 1908 Olympics, John Hayes from the United States won the marathon. He had earned his place on the Olympic team by finishing first in the Yonkers Marathon and second in the Boston Marathon. He was a salesman at Bloomingdale's department store in New York City and after he qualified for the Olympic team, the store had a cinder track built on the roof so that he could run his 10 miles a day after work.

Hayes actually finished the Olympic Marathon in second place. His time had been 2:58:18, 32 seconds behind Dorando Pietri of Italy. However, ABC's film clip showed what had been described by *The New York Times*: "Pietri staggering like a drunken man, as he slowly tottered down the home stretch. Three times he fell, struggled to his feet, and each time, aided by track officials, he fought his way toward the tape." The help that the officials gave Pietri, or Dorando as he came to be called by the press, caused him to be disqualified and Hayes became the winner.

The front-page coverage given by the American newspapers caused a sensation in the United States. Promoters invited Dorando to the United States for a race in Madison Square Garden with Hayes. *The New York Times* described what happened: "The immense hall was filled completely . . . with attendance from every class, from the gallery gods to the patrons of the first nights . . ." After 262 laps had been run around the inside of the Garden making 26 miles, "a riot was all but precipitated by the thoughtless holders of arena box seats, who in the mistaken idea that the race had ended, hurried from their boxes when the race still had two more laps to run. The police moved into the melee . . . blows were struck and fighting sprung up on every side. Dorando carried on to finish the race and win by nearly half a lap in 2:44. . . ." Dorando received the first-place prize money of $3,000 and Hayes with his winnings retired from Bloomingdale's.

Shortly after the Hayes-Pietri marathon the 1908 Yonkers Marathon was held. It started at Yonkers' Getty Square, where five thousand people gathered to watch the start. From there the course curved northward to Tarrytown, New York, and then returned to Yonkers along the Hudson River, the last 8 miles offering one torturous hill after another. It is believed to be the most difficult marathon course in the United States. The finish of the marathon was at the Empire City Track and the leader, Jim Crowley, ran the last 4 miles before some twenty thousand people. As had happened in Madison Square Garden, the crowd poured onto the track as he finished. This brought an abrupt end to the race because the rest of the runners couldn't get around the track. There were too many people in the way. No times or places were recorded for the rest of the field of 150 runners.

In April, 1909, promoters staged the "Marathon Derby" at the Polo Grounds in New York. Dorando, Hayes and a Frenchman, Henri St. Yves, were invited, among others. St. Yves, who was only 4'11" in height, was a waiter in London, and as *The New York Times* put it, "virtually despised in the betting" by the twenty-five thousand people who had paid up to $20 a ticket. St. Yves ran the first mile in 5:14, and 5 miles in 28 minutes, which brought an end to the scoffing. At

20 miles his time was 1:57, despite the rain-soaked, muddy course. At the finish, reached in 2:40, a new world record, the New York Sixty-Ninth Regiment Band and Viola's Italian Band played "Le Marseillaise," and the crowd gave him a standing ovation. For his efforts, St. Yves received $5,000. Dorando finished second in 2:45 and Hayes third in 2:48. The "Marathon Derby" finally settled the rivalry between John Hayes and Dorando Pietri, and the marathon fever, aroused by the 1908 Olympic Marathon subsided.

At the end of the television break Shorter was still running in the English Garden along the rutted, serpentine paths that wind through the park's woods, lawns and flower beds, past picnic pavilions, along the banks of streams and a lake. . . . Keep up the pace . . . cut off the corner of the path . . . straighten twist out . . . quads tight, using too much toe . . . more heel . . . hamstrings smooth . . . no catches . . . all alone . . . no noise . . . silence . . . cool shade . . . cold cold . . . back wet, stiff . . . drop hands, shrug . . . pace has slowed . . . more lift, pick up notch . . . they have lost all contact . . . dispiriting for them . . . can't know what it takes to catch me . . . stiffness in back . . . work against it . . . keep smooth . . . ruts . . . ruts . . . watch out . . . blue line . . . cut corner off . . . feel rhythm . . . stiffness not bad . . . move over people blocking path . . . clap clap . . . baby carriage . . . smile . . . clap clap clap clap . . . clap . . . fade out . . . alone . . . green banks grassy . . . canal . . . green canal . . . ducks . . . swans . . . glide . . . smooth . . . flowing . . . no adrenaline . . . pick up pace . . . concentrate . . . keep on it . . . cut off corner . . . get over . . . back again to other side . . . tangent running . . . silence . . . quiet . . . push down diaphragm relax . . . path straight now . . . relax, feel

rhythm . . . smooth smooth float . . . coming to turn . . . keep
straight line, cut corner, drop shoulders . . . back to other side,
shorten stride . . . like cross-country . . . people ahead . . . can
hear clapping . . . press . . . police cars . . . left turn . . . clap
clap . . . clap fade . . . dust . . . ruts . . . bicycle tire ruts . . . Mt.
Hermon track . . . remember frozen ruts . . . Miruts Yifter . . .
53 seconds twenty-fifth quarter . . . head down . . . watch for
footing on path . . . Wolde's head down . . . has a kick too . . .
57 last quarter . . . watch pace . . . 5 miles in garden . . . 20
quarters at 72 seconds . . . try to feel pace . . . only fatigue . . .
weak . . . pace too fast . . . relax . . . Chinese tower tier on top
of tier, pagoda roof layer cake . . . Yusami . . . what happened
to him? Look back . . . can't see, trees . . . coming to aid station . . . push to . . . don't linger . . . keep going . . . bottle 1014
. . . my bottle . . . there 1014 . . . grab it . . . suck it in . . . relax
gut . . . move . . . move . . . bottle in mouth . . . suck, squeeze
. . . bend over, relax diaphragm . . . get going . . . pick it up,
losing time on garden paths . . . can't lose more . . . push . . .
legs are too tight from path, use more heel . . . work them out
. . . relax . . . down diaphragm, breathe deeply . . . lake . . .
rowboats . . . flags . . Seehaus Cafe been there . . . people . . .
dog barking, he's coming at me . . . get off on grass . . . clap
clap . . . laughter . . . nicht sprechen Sie deutsch . . . can't
understand them . . . Wolde's kick . . . thirty-nine years old . . .
like Yifter old, nobody knows how old . . . has kick, stronger
at end of race . . . hang on . . . don't slow . . . pain blurrrrr . . .
left shoulder hurts . . . bad patch will pass . . . relax shake
shoulder out, move it around, drop it down . . . slowing . . .
get back stride . . . keep form, strength is in form . . . no
strength, just form . . . all in knee lift lift, drive them forward
. . . toe-point . . . hang on . . . God how far? . . . can't be much

to 35 K . . . nearly out of park . . . path winding . . . straighten it out . . . cut off corners . . . weaving all over the place . . . one curve after another . . . coming to end of park . . . Hordes of people . . . God, the people . . . water station coming . . . keep pace to first table . . . don't walk . . . here it is . . . my bottle? . . . 1014 . . . got it . . . move . . . get moving . . . squeeze it out, makes me sick . . . got to drink . . . enough, throw it away . . . clap clap . . . shouts, "Go U.S." . . . people . . . kids' hands out . . . faces . . . slowing down, down, concentrate on pace, knee lift . . . television guy holding up two fingers, 2 minutes . . . does he know? . . . close at least . . . my God, they can't catch me . . . only if I cramp up . . . keep form . . . ease off a notch . . . crowd makes adrenaline . . . don't get carried away . . . hamstrings can cramp up and blow it . . . breathing too forced, ease off . . . just maintain . . . push down diaphragm . . . shake out shoulders . . . relax belly . . . faces faces faces . . . clap clap clap clap clap clap . . . deafening racket . . . flapbapflapbapflapbapflap . . . helicopters . . . people, people, police holding back people, barricades . . . hang on . . . no need with this lead . . . gotta keep form, shorten stride protect hamstrings . . . can take anything else . . . can't feel anything. Too much . . . hang on . . . feet numb . . . weak . . . slowing . . . hang on, keep leg speed hang on on on on . . . "35 kilometers" white letters in road . . . time? time? . . . refreshment station coming . . . pace pace pace . . . work out shoulder drop shoulder, hands down, asphalt black smooth . . . pick up knees, up, leg exchange . . . blurrrrrrrrrr . . . pain blurs out . . . hang on . . . wooden tables, bottles, bottles . . . 1014 there . . . can't drink, sickening, take some, squeeze . . . more . . . sickening . . . dropped it . . . slowed . . . go, move . . . less than 5 K to go, thank God . . . keep pace on incline . . .

pace pace pace pace, maintain maintain maintain smooth smooth smooth . . . can see stadium . . . blurrrrrrrrrr hang on on onononononon blurrrrrrrr . . . flapbapflapbapflapbap . . . red light on-off on-off . . . pedestrian bridge . . . blurrrrrrrr . . . stadium, not much further blurrrrr, hamstrings O.K. . . . blurrrrrr . . . blapblapblapblapblap army helicopter . . . blurrr . . . people people people, clap clap clap clap . . . blurrrr . . . hang onto it, no trouble, hang on, keep smooth . . . hold on. Feet numb . . . hold on . . . pace pace pace pace . . . blurrrrrrrr . . . look back, too stiff . . . blurrrrrr . . . "40 kilometers" white letters . . . stadium coming, 2 kilometers left . . . keep pace . . . cold waves . . . cold . . . hang on . . . blurrrrrrrr . . . "41 kilometers" . . . stadium . . . red light on-off on-off . . . bus stopped . . . on-off on-off . . . bus turning off . . . hold onto pace, hold on . . . I've done it . . . police . . . stadium tunnel . . . people behind barricades . . . soldiers . . . tunnel entrance . . .

All of the television viewers are waiting for Shorter to come through the tunnel under the stadium. Erich Segal is ecstatic. But the cameras show another runner coming out of the tunnel onto the track. It isn't Shorter. Segal shouts: "That's not Frank!"

McKay says: "The man who came into the stadium isn't Frank Shorter."

Segal: "The guy is an imposter! That used to happen in the Boston Marathon. That's an imposter. Get him off the track!"

McKay: "It looks like a fake in the Olympic Games. They ought to throw him out."

Shorter is seen coming out of the tunnel and onto the track.

Segal shouts: "You won Frank. You won."

The imposter had waited in the tunnel until he saw Shorter coming and then went out onto the track and ran to the finish line about a hundred yards ahead of Shorter.

The television viewers saw Shorter take his victory lap around the stadium waving in response to the crowd's cheering which poured out when they realized that Shorter was the winner and they had cheered for another. The stadium's giant digital clock had caught him breaking the tape in 2:12:19.8. Karl Lismont, a tiny, pale ghost of a man dressed all in white, sped onto the track pushing the pace, to finish in 2:14:31, followed by a frail little black man. It was Mamo Wolde who had been passed earlier by Lismont. He finished in 2:15:08. Then came Kenny Moore struggling and running on a "cushion of blisters." Back in the English Garden his hamstring muscles in the back of his right thigh had cramped, and Wolde, with whom he had been running, went on ahead. While Moore was trying to work out the cramp Lismont overtook him. Once out of the park and back onto the asphalt Moore's hamstrings smoothed out, he got back his rhythm and picked up the pace. He finished in 2:15:39 and was caught by Shorter, who was waiting for him. Arms around each other they walked off on the infield grass. Forty-seven seconds later Kimihara from Japan came driving over the line, followed in succession by Jack Batcheler, Derek Clayton, Jack Foster, and Gaston Roelants.

Shorter was the first American to win the Olympic Marathon since Johnny Hayes did it in 1908. When asked what his thoughts were upon finishing, Shorter said that he had only a great feeling of thankfulness that the thing was over and that he wouldn't have to do it again for a while. After the awards ceremonies he went to Abebe Bikila and shook his hand. Bikila's 1964 Olympic Marathon time of 2:12:11 still stood as the Olympic record, Shorter's time being slower by 8 seconds. Shorter said later that when he came onto the stadium track and saw the clock he thought that he could break Bikila's record by running hard, but decided not to because that would be "hot dogging," so he just maintained pace to the finish. Shorter's race was not against Bikila and breaking his record was not a goal.

The conditioning of the mind in marathon running is as important as the condition of the body. As Shorter so often has put it, "I didn't know whether or not my mind was willing to put my body through it." When he said this, he was referring to the last third of the marathon, particularly the last 6 miles, which is often said to be the "last half of the race." When a runner fails to keep the pace, slows down, stops and walks, and it isn't because of illness, cramps or injury, it is because his mind has "cracked." His determination and will power have been broken by a rebellious body whose messages to slow down or stop are acted upon. As Shorter has often put it, the last miles are "a fight not to slow down." It is a fight between the body and the mind. Which of them will win is largely a matter of strength of the mind's will power. Motivation is a strengthener of will power, and the Olympic Games provide great motivation. Nothing else in the way of competition comes close to providing the impetus of the Olympics. All over the world athletes in the various Olympic disciplines train for years just for the games. Shorter was not alone in his magnificent obsession.

Other motivational forces were at work that day in Munich. Fear of heat and humidity, for the combination of heat and humidity can quickly destroy a marathon runner. The problem posed by heat and humidity is that a runner sweats out more in perspiration than he can take in and becomes dehydrated. This causes his muscles to function badly and cramps to set in.

Hill, Wolde, Lismont, Clayton, Moore, and Yusami let Shorter get away from them at about 9 miles because they feared the heat and humidity more than they feared him. It was too early in the race and the pace had not been that fast for them to have let him go, but fear held them back. They did not take the risk of being wrecked by dehydration. Shorter took the gamble. He knew what cards he held: his past training in the heat of Florida and New Mexico; his lack of body fat which helps his system keep itself cool; his darkness in coloration which enables him to handle the heat. The point at which he begins to feel cold, 60 degrees, most marathoners feel is already too warm by at least 10 degrees. Shorter knows his body very well.

Shorter also knows the psychological aspects of marathon running, evidenced by his use of the tactic of "breaking away." He did what he had to do to get away from the rest of the field. But he didn't start trying to break away until after the first third of the race had been cruised through, because first he had to protect himself from the most destructive element of all, the 26 miles. Breaking away means getting a substantial lead on your competitors. That could be less than 50 yards when two runners are going one-on-one in the latter stages of the race. Ultimately it means getting away to the point where visual contact is broken. The reason for Shorter's breaking away was to leave a sense of defeat with the runners left behind and a feeling that they are left to run for the remaining medals. As the gap increases, so does the strength of these feelings.

The emotion generated in Shorter when he broke contact with the field also had the effect of propelling him. His running all alone enabled him to work out his own rhythm and pace which he prefers to do, and it gave him a whiff of sweet victory. It made him feel that he was being chased. Chased by the specters of the best in the world whom he held in awe for their accomplishments. He feared losing ground to any one of them, knowing that all would be very tough if they ever caught up with him. It was constantly on his mind that at least one of them would get his act together and come after him.

Shorter's victory at Munich, together with ABC's television coverage of it, turned his name into a household word. His picture was on one magazine cover after another and he was on all of the talk shows. The press could not get enough of him. Middletown, New York, his old hometown, gave him and his wife Louise a key to the city.

T.B.

(CONTINUED)

Frank Shorter

ELECTROGLYDE IN BLUE
AND GOLD

SHORTER took the first step on the road to the Olympics in Munich when he was waiting to take his last exam at Yale before graduation in June 1969. He had time on his hands and went to his track coach Bob Giegengack and asked him what he thought Shorter could accomplish as a runner if he "really worked at it." Shorter had not been great in college as a miler or 2-miler. He had difficulty winning even in the Ivy League. But Giegengack gave him the most valuable commodity a coach has to give, and that is encouragement. He told Shorter that he could make the Olympic team and even win a gold medal, "if he really worked at it."

This strong encouragement was given because Shorter had the speed for the 10,000-meter (6.2 miles), but he had

43

never shown the endurance to maintain a world class pace for that distance. At Yale, his running had not caused shortfalls in his academic or in his social life. He liked to drink beer and to sing with a group called "The Bachelors." His love of singing had carried over from his younger years while at St. John the Divine Choir School in New York City.

Giegengack's encouragement fueled Shorter's curiosity to find out just how good he could be. He knew that to have a chance of becoming world class, twice a day workouts would be necessary to get in the heavy, quality mileage needed to build up endurance to maintain the pace. Running twice a day a total of from 15 to 20 miles, however, soon changes a person into a runner. Anything else he may have been before takes a distant second. But he had until that September to experiment with his running before he would begin medical school at the University of New Mexico. Becoming a doctor had long been a goal. His father and grandfather were both doctors in Middletown, New York. Grandfather Shorter, an eye doctor, had a sign outside of his office: "See Shorter, See Longer."

Shorter's daily double workouts did wonders. Within a month's time he had the endurance needed to win the NCAA (National Collegiate Athletic Association) 6-mile National Championship. He said that two workouts a day had the effect of reducing his recovery time: that is, he had less time to recover from one workout to the next. The shorter the time interval between workouts the heavier the stress and the heavier the stress, the greater the training effect. However, to counterbalance the stress of the double workouts, he had to have a lot of sleep, ten or eleven hours a night.

The transformation that took place in Shorter between the time he spoke with Giegengack and his winning the

NCAA championship was similar to the transformation that had taken place while he was at Mt. Hermon School in Massachusetts. There he went from eightieth in his class in his junior year to third by the time he was graduated. He saw that he was not going to get into Yale the way he was going and went to work to pick himself up. Kenny Moore said of him: "Frank does whatever he has to, whatever is needed. Ultimately, he even won a gold medal that way." Of himself Shorter has said, "I was always predicted to underachieve but I always got by. If one approach doesn't work, I'll try another and I have the confidence that it will work out."

After he was graduated from Yale, he started that September in medical school at the University of New Mexico.

In November, however he dropped out because of a family financial crisis. The savings of the large Shorter family (Frank is second oldest of ten children) had become exhausted. Frank returned home for a while, then he went to Gainesville, Florida, where a fine runner and friend Jack Batcheler lived. He joined the Florida track club and started training with Jack. His pursuit of finding out how good he could become continued. He said in *Runners World*: "It became a matter of singular concentration, discipline, monomania. I had to zero in on one thing. I had to make it so nothing else mattered. The distance runner always knows how good he is because he knows the distance he runs, the strength he has. He can't hide anything from himself. He always has the feeling of 'If I worked harder I could have been. . .' I just made up my mind to work and see how good I could be. I didn't want to quit and say for the rest of my life. 'Well, maybe I could have been.'"

In Jack Batcheler, Frank had a kindred spirit. Jack was a

graduate student in entomology and had been on the Olympic 5,000-meter team in 1968, but had the misfortune of becoming ill after having qualified for the finals, and did not run. The two of them managed to run quite a bit together, despite their keeping different hours. Jack, a morning person, liked to start his first workout at six in the morning and Shorter, a night person, liked to start later, around eleven. Shorter told *Runners World* of their training together: "Most of our long stuff we ran together—except when I didn't get up at 6 o'clock to meet Jack as he came pattering back like clockwork. This was more often than not because I like to drink beer and sleep late but Jack doesn't do much of either.

". . . We worked hard. But everybody works hard . . . I'd say we average about 20–24 miles a day. He runs a little more than I do. This is a training day when there's no meet coming up. I run interval workouts, I run a morning workout. This is about 140 miles a week, with three interval workouts included . . .

"If someone were to ask me my pace, I couldn't tell them. I don't know how fast we run. Before I went down to Florida, I used to run between 5:10 and 5:30 miles for about 5 or 6 miles. I'd really burn. Remember, I'd come in and tell you, Jack, that I'd just run 5 or 6 miles at 5:30 pace. Jack would say, 'Oh, O.K.' And Jack would go pitter-patter, pitter-patter on his runs. Finally I said, hell, O.K. And I went out pitter-patter, pitter-patter. Just running how it's comfortable!'"

The heavy stress needed for conditioning of the body results in a corresponding need for rest, rest which you never seem to get quite enough of. Why, one asks, would anybody put himself through this. Shorter has said that to him running is "a sensual experience." He loves it and dreads having to take a day off to nurse an injury. He said in the *New York Times Magazine*: "You simply cannot be a distance runner if you're goal-oriented. Most of the swimmers at Munich said they never wanted to see the pool again once their race was over. Most of the distance runners, on the other hand, were on the track the next day. I did 5 miles the morning after the marathon, and 20 the day after that."

It seems evident, however, that he not only loves to run but also loves to have a goal, a purpose for the training. A few years ago he said that in five years of running he had only missed six days. Even when he has the flu he gets himself out of bed in the afternoon, fever and all, for a run. He has worked out running routes around many of the world's airports that he uses in his traveling.

In an afternoon's training run out on the roads with friends, Shorter often pushes the pace down below 70 seconds a quarter. He also has it pushed against him, by some great runners, like Herb Lindsay, who have moved to Boulder, Colorado and are working for him in the store he owns there. Lindsay ran the 1980 Trevira 10-miler on a very hilly course in New York City's Central Park in 45:59.8, just under a 4:36 per mile.

Rare is the day when Shorter doesn't push himself or isn't pushed close to the limit. When he went out to Eugene, Oregon, to visit Kenny Moore, he used to run with Steve Prefontaine who lived and went to college there. An afternoon's training run of 15 miles was usual for Shorter when in marathon training, but longer by about 5 miles than what Pre liked to do. Pre's longest racing distance was 5,000 meters, so his training runs were shorter. On the road Pre liked to use a 6-

minute pace like Shorter, but when Shorter pushed, the faster pace, plus the longer distance, brought on all kinds of sputtering from Pre.

In 1973, the two met in the 3-mile Bowerman Classic, with Shorter a stand-in for Lasse Viren who was injured. The race had been planned to give Pre another shot at Viren who had beaten him in the 5,000-meter at Munich in 1972. The 12-lap battle was tough for both Prefontaine and Shorter. In the last lap, Shorter surged ahead and held a 10-yard lead with only 220 yards to go. With 80 yards left, Pre came up to Shorter's shoulder and from there the two went head to head. Pre took it by a second in 12:51, a new American record.

His goal was eventually to run a 12:36, the world record, before he retired. He didn't have time to make it. He was killed behind the wheel of his gold-colored MG having run off the road one night in a never fully understood accident. Shorter was one of the last people to see him the evening of his death.

In *The Runner*, Shorter said of Pre: "He was somebody I held in awe, not for the time he ran, but for the way he ran. All out. Steve did not really associate with me in a close personal manner until his last year, after I shared the lead with him at the Bowerman Classic 3-Mile. Then, it was as if I had passed some sort of test, and I guess in Steve's eyes, I had because he had high expectations for others as well as for himself . . . He thought it was only right I should help him with the pace. I did and that was that. I was his friend."

The constant training, Shorter thinks, brings strength, durability, endurance. As the German philosopher Friedrich Nietzsche put it, "What does not kill me makes me stronger." The more you push yourself, the tougher you will become.

However, without rest the stress will soon make a wreck of you. Shorter said in an interview with John Jerome in *Outside* magazine:

"Your body, no matter how you train it, is only capable of standing so much stress, then you have to let it rest. Beyond a certain point the training effect is not going to be able to make you withstand a maximum effort any better. You can get faster, but you can't withstand the maximum effort any better. For me, it's hard to do a marathon more than about twice a year. Three times a year is about maximum. You tear yourself down in the ways that are yet to be measured. I don't train too specifically for distances. I train mostly for the 10,000 meters, and just run marathons. If you're training marathon distances all the time, you are so torn down that you can't do the kind of speed training you need to be able to run fast."

Incorporated in his training Shorter does a great deal of speed work on a track. They are called interval workouts. In the *New York Times Magazine* he told of one of his great interval workouts: "Three times a week I do interval work in addition to distance. That means sprinting, short rest, sprinting again. Once I did more than I had ever done before: I had done nine 6-minute miles in the morning, and then, in the afternoon, a 3-mile warmup. Then the intervals: 15 quarter-miles that averaged around 61 seconds each with a 50-yard jog in between. Which is to say, almost no rest at all. Until then I'd never done intervals with less than 100 yards of rest. Until then, too, I'd never averaged out under 64 seconds. When I got to the fifteenth quarter that day, I was empty. But suddenly, out of nowhere, God, I still don't know where I got it, I did a 58-second quarter." Shainberg, who was doing the interview, said of Shorter, "He paused and looked at me. There was a kind of intensity that I had never seen in his eyes before. 'Fifty-eight seconds—do you understand? After 15 quarters at 61. I don't think anyone's ever done that before!'"

Shorter's double daily workouts, with track intervals three times a week, gave him the endurance needed to hold a 5-minute pace over a long distance and to go even faster over short distances. Until the 1970 Drake Relays, his best time for 3 miles was 13:43. There he ran 13:15 and finished second to Jack Batcheler. At the Drake Relays in 1971, he ran and won in 13:06. The next day, he won a 6-miler in 27:24. These back-to-back wins indicated to him that he might have attained a level of endurance fitness needed for a marathon. Two months later, he entered the marathon trials for the Pan American Games. Kenny Moore also entered. In that race, Shorter stayed with Moore through 23 miles, but Moore then broke away and went on to win. Shorter's time was 2:17. A month later, in Cali, Colombia, at high altitude and in 90-degree heat, Shorter won the Pan Am Games Marathon, even though he had to make a diarrhea stop. His time was 2:22, 4 minutes ahead of Moore, who was second. Shorter also won the 10,000-meter race.

On the strength of these wins, he was invited to run in the 1971 Fukuoka Marathon to be held in November. Kenny Moore who had finished second the year before also was invited. The Fukuoka Marathon has been considered since 1966 to be the unofficial world championship. Only the best in the world have been invited to run there. They usually come because all their expenses are paid and they receive great treatment, as would visiting royalty—limousines, tours, banquets, an avalanche of gifts, the most prized of which are custom-made Tiger shoes. The winner of the Fukuoka becomes a national hero in Japan. The Fukuoka is held on an out-and-back course, with the turnaround point coming at 13.1 miles. Moore wrote in *Sports Illustrated*: "Several hundred yards after turning for home, he [Shorter] met me laboring among the stragglers. 'Put it to them,' I said, needlessly. There was blood in his eye and he was running with a light, driving precision.

"With 9 miles to go, Frank had gained 200 yards on Yusami and Foster, who were running together. The crowd changed in tone. Applause for Frank was warm, but the resounding encouragement behind him was of a different order. He used it to gauge his lead. 'The race is always between 20 and 26 miles,' he said later. 'My only doubt was that my mind was ready to put my body through that. When I got into it, I still didn't know. There was the pain, and there was a peculiar frustration. I can run a 4-minute mile. It was agonizing for a runner like me to not be able to do anything but crawl.'

"They ran the last 3 miles into the teeth of the wind. The gritty, powerful Yusami shook off Foster and drove on after Frank.

" 'It was the hardest I've ever run,' said Frank. 'Even in the heat of Cali, I felt better. Here, I was so helpless.'

"He won by 32 seconds in 2:12:50.4."

" 'I finished and a great feeling of thankfulness swept through me. There was no sense of conquest, none of this baloney about vanquishing anybody.'

"Across the line, he waved away blankets and fought off officials and reporters to stand at the finish and embrace Yusami.

" 'My only thought was, "Here we are, goddamn it! We made it!" This man had suffered as much as I had. We all had.' "

The Fukuoka Marathon is sponsored by the Asahi Shimbun, a newspaper chain, and they subject the runners to interviews for their papers. In one of them, Shorter, when asked about the pain of a marathon, said, according to Kenny Moore in *Sports Illustrated*, "You have to forget your last marathon before you run another. Your mind knows what's coming."

Shorter distinguishes between pain for which you get medical treatment and the pain incurred in running a marathon. To find out about the pain of a marathon, he suggested that interviewer Shainberg go out and run twice a day for a year and when he got up to 15 miles a day, come back and discuss the matter again. Anybody who runs 15 miles a day will become acquainted with the kind of pain experienced in a marathon. It comes when you push your body down the road when there is no energy left and the muscles are stiff and unyielding. All the messages to the brain are to stop. This is not the pain of an injury, like the stress fracture Abebe Bikila suffered in the 1968 Olympic Marathon. For that kind of thing you stop and get help. But the pain from muscle stiffness and depletion of the body's glycogen fuel is another thing. Rather than pain, extreme discomfort describes it better, because the runner can go on without doing any harm. In fact, he will be strengthening and expanding his metabolism capabilities by getting his system used to shifting from the metabolism of glycogen to the metabolism of fat, of which the body has almost an unlimited supply.

Fifteen miles a day will put anyone, including Shorter, in a state of at least mild depletion in a short time because it takes more than twenty-four hours to recover the glycogen expended in a 15-mile run. As a result of being forced to run in a glycogen-depleted state, the body will adjust to burning fat, which is not as efficient as burning glycogen. It requires more oxygen. This increased demand for oxygen to metabolize fat is a real troublemaker for world class marathoners like Shorter. Shorter's pace for the last 9 miles of the Munich Olympic Marathon averaged 4:49 a mile. His system can, however, only take in and distribute enough oxygen for his muscles down to a rate of 5:30 a mile. So when he runs out of glycogen at about 20 miles into the marathon and his system has only fat to burn, the increased shortage in the supply of oxygen results in an even greater increase in the production of lactic acid, and this lactic acid causes his muscles to stiffen up.

Shorter uses track interval workouts to set up the situation in which his muscles get overloaded with lactic acid. Continuing to run quarters in a muscle-stiffened state gets him ready to run that way in races.

Shorter follows only in part a practice that is used by many marathoners to increase the glycogen stored in their muscles and liver in advance of a race. The practice is called carbohydrate loading. It involves eating little or no carbohydrates for a few days to deplete oneself almost completely of glycogen. Then about three days before the race, the runner eats nothing but carbohydrates. As a result of the depletion, the muscles and liver will overcompensate once they get the carbohydrates, storing up more of it than they would normally. During the three days of carbo-loading the runner does little in the way of training, so as not to diminish the store before the race.

Shorter says that he does not go on the depletion part of

the diet, because he is already depleted most of the time from the heavy mileage. He does stay away from protein, however, during the last few days before a race.

Shorter's anaerobic threshold is reached as he goes below the 5:30 a mile pace. He can carry on a normal conversation, without shortness of breath, until then. When he has a business meeting with some of his partners out on the road he is the only one left talking after a few miles. His maximum oxygen uptake is 7.1 liters, in layman's shorthand. Steve Prefontaine was tested at 8.7, the highest uptake of any runner ever tested in the United States. Bill Rodgers was tested at Ball State University and found to have a 7.8 capacity. In simple terms, oxygen uptake is the capacity of a person's system to take in oxygen, which the lungs accomplish, and transport it, which the blood's hemoglobin (the oxygen-carrying component of red blood cells) does, to the muscle cells. There it is burned with glycogen and fat to produce energy which enables the muscle to do its work.

The faster the pace, the greater the demand for oxygen by the muscles, and the demand for oxygen by the muscles increases not as the pace increases, but in an exponential progression, oxygen $=$ velocity^3. For example, if a runner needs 2 liters of oxygen at a 10-minute pace, he will need, not 4 liters at a 5-minute pace, but rather, 8 liters.

Shorter's oxygen uptake is not high compared to many other world class runners; however, it is higher than Derek Clayton's 6.9 liters. Since the ability to take in and distribute oxygen is about the most limiting factor any runner faces, particularly a marathon runner, the question raised by this is how Clayton and Shorter can have done so well against others with higher uptakes. Both, it seems, have compensating factors which offset the lack of superiority in their cardiovascular systems. They have an ability to use a higher percentage (over 85 percent) of their oxygen-uptake capacity. Each also has a very efficient running style, although entirely different from one another's. Clayton's style keeps him very close to the ground; Shorter's is very buoyant. What seems to be the most important factor is that both Shorter and Clayton trained at a very high level of intensity. This resulted in an adaptation by the body to operating efficiently at high levels of intensity. Clayton's training pace approached 5 minutes per mile, the fastest training pace for any great marathoner, and Shorter's was not far behind.

An additional compensating factor is that the muscles in Shorter's legs contain a great deal more of "fast twitch" muscle fiber than most marathoners. Sprinters' muscles contain an abundance of fast twitch fibers. They are white in color, like those in a chicken wing, and differ from slow twitch muscle fiber which is dark in color, like those in a chicken leg. The result seems to be that Shorter's consumption of oxygen is less because of the preponderance of fast twitch muscle fiber which requires less oxygen.

Shorter eats only one decent meal a day, consuming mostly junk food the rest of the time. His hand is never far from a bag of M&Ms and a coffee cup or a bottle of Coke. The Olympia beer that is consumed in considerable quantity, he calls his "secret electrolyte replacement." His real meal does not come until the end of the day. Since he will run after breakfast, he cannot eat very much. A dish of Cheerios and a cup of coffee is about all that he can eat and still run. Shorter's lunch doesn't amount to much either, because of his afternoon workout; a piece of layer cake, Coke, and a candy bar will tide him over.

His eating habits appear to be bizarre. But his running leaves him so depleted of glycogen his system craves foods that will quickly pick up his blood sugar level. That is to say he eats the kind of food that his body demands. The real nutrition is supplied by his one decent meal of meat and vegetables at night. Studies have shown that the German people, just after the end of World War II, when they were close to starving, were much healthier than they are today. The average German was then getting less than half of the calories that he gets today. It may be said that what Shorter doesn't eat is what makes him so healthy.

Shorter was one of the first in the United States to understand the benefits resulting from living and training at high altitudes where the oxygen in the air is thin. The oxygen taken into the blood stream is transported by the hemoglobin, which is a component of the red blood cells. The human system will adjust to an increase in altitude by increasing the amount of hemoglobin in the blood, so that it can transport more oxygen. This compensating adaptation requires about two weeks to complete. Most marathons are held at or near sea level, rather than in the mountains. So when Shorter comes down from Boulder, Colorado, which is about 5,400 feet above sea level, his blood will contain a high hemoglobin count. Because his red blood cell and hemoglobin count are so important, he must take care to take in enough iron in what he eats, because iron is the main component of hemoglobin and he, like many runners, has a tendency towards anemia. The hemoglobin count is so important that distance runners getting ready for the Olympics will head for the mountains

(Lasse Viren went to Bogota, Colombia, before the 1980 games in Moscow).

After the 1976 games in Montreal, Viren was questioned, as were other runners from Europe, about the matter of "blood-doping." That involves taking a runner's blood and then transfusing it back into him before the race. Neither Viren nor any other runner has admitted to having done it, however. The East Germans, who are the leaders in the world today in sports medicine, have gone so far into the matter of blood chemistry for their athletes that they have computerized each athlete's blood chemistry records. If a runner, for example, has a bad race or workout, the trainer takes a blood sample, does a blood chemistry, puts the results into the computer and finds out immediately how the athlete's training should be varied to rectify the poor performance. Many believe that the training of the great runners of the future will be largely in the hands of the biochemists.

"The vertical hyphen" description of Shorter, attributed to Marti Liquori, fits perfectly, because Shorter seems to lean neither forward nor backwards. He tries to stay upright, in the Bowerman style, because leaning forward cuts down on his forward leg extension, and leaning backward reduces the power of his trailing leg. The power in Shorter's trailing leg, as seen on film in slow motion, passes down his back through his butt, into his leg that is driven straight, then to his foot which is cocked like a spring and released when it hits the ground. His foot pops off the pavement about 6 inches, leaving his toes pointed vertically. This thrust upwards lifts him off the ground. It gives him the "Shorter float." The power which is transmitted down through his foot and the shock of its landing on the road time after time has taken its toll, leaving him with twisted and gnarled feet. At 120 miles per week, it is estimated that each foot strikes and thrusts off of the pavement upwards of 4 million times per year.

His feet receive a ritual of care: a winding of a tissue-thin foam rubber called pre-tape that protects the feet from the blisters that the adhesive tape can cause, then foam rubber metatarsal pads, all of which are bound up with yards of adhesive tape that go around and around the foot, covering his arch. He does this twice a day, before each run. Orthotics, or arch supports, have not worked for him. Aside from the tape and pads, the only concession he makes to his feet are the wearing of training shoes with thicker soles, when he is not racing. These, like his racing shoes, are made by Tiger in Japan.

His racing shoes are about the same as those you can buy in a running store and are called Ohbori, named after a park in Fukuoka, but they are custom-made to the measure of his long and narrow foot. Recently these shoes have come into the running shoe stores with a heavier sole than the old Ohbori shoes, and are named "XBR," short for Experimental Bill Rodgers. Shorter's racing shoes are little more than track shoes without spikes. The soles are cut out under the arch, giving little or no support there or anyplace else. In the narrow heel there is only one-half inch of foam rubber covered with a thin latex covering to provide traction. In the forefoot they are only about three-eighths of an inch thick, providing very little in the way of cushioning, but also very little in the way of weight.

The long-distance running increases the strength of Shorter's posterial muscles while doing little or nothing for the anterior muscles, and this leads to an imbalance which causes problems particularly in the lower back and lower leg. To prevent this imbalance, stretching of the posterior muscles is necessary along with strengthening the anterior muscles. Shorter follows a simple set of exercises that he has found suitable; sitting on the floor, or standing up, with legs spread and bending over at the waist toward each leg, while keeping the knees locked. This exercise stretches the lower back muscles and the hamstrings in the back of the thighs. For his calves and Achilles tendons, he will lean against a wall, keeping his knees locked and heels on the floor. Without these stretches he would probably have suffered the same fate as did Derek Clayton before he saw the light and started stretching. Clayton had to go through some nine surgical operations, which greatly shortened his competitive career. Before he started stretching, Clayton's only warmup used to be on the road with two slow 7-minute miles. When he finished his run he never stretched, just took a shower. He said that he used to get so tight that he could not even touch his knees.

Shorter has had his difficulties with tightness despite stretching. In his left lower leg a tight muscle pulling on a ligament eventually pulled the ligament away from the bone to which it was attached and with it came a piece of the bone. Thereafter calcification took place at the rupture point. On April 26, 1978, Shorter was operated on by Dr. Stan James, an orthopedic surgeon practicing in Eugene, Oregon, with a depth of experience in runners' problems. The operation was successful. In July of that year Shorter ran again for the first time—two 10-minute miles. It was a joyous occasion for him.

Shorter reigned supreme in the world of marathoning

from November 1971 until the middle of April 1975, during which time he won the Fukuoka Marathon four times in a row. In the 1975 Boston Marathon, Bill Rodgers surfaced for the first time in top-level marathoning. Rodgers's intention in that race was to improve on his previous best time of 2:19:34, but by the halfway point he had broken away from the field. At Heartbreak Hill, about 16 miles, he gave up nearly a half minute of his lead retying a shoelace, and then, in the next 10 miles stopped twice more to drink water. Despite his stopping he won in 2:09:55, breaking Shorter's record of 2:10:30, set at Fukuoka in 1972. When he heard his time, Rodgers couldn't believe it and said, "I can't run that fast." It was more than 9.5 minutes faster than his previous best.

In 1975 Shorter's best marathon was a 2:16:29, but as the 1976 Olympics loomed on the horizon he decided to go again and began the intense drive to get in shape. One 140-mile week followed another. Some weeks he averaged more than 20 miles a day. At the trials Shorter and Rodgers ran away with the race, and were together until the last few miles, when Shorter turned on his speed and went on to beat Rodgers by 7 seconds, in the time of 2:11:51. The race for the third spot on the team went to Don Kardong who at the end outsprinted Tony Sandoval.

The 1976 Summer Olympic Games were held in Montreal, Canada. Shorter was the favorite in the marathon, and all the runners were keying on him, in particular Waldemar Cierpinski, an East German who tried to keep physical contact with him, constantly touching his shoulder or arm. An aggravating tactic, it is often used in track races in Europe, but not in marathons. Kenny Moore said that when he and Mamo Wolde were running together in the 1972 Olympic

Marathon, Wolde would always ask to be excused when he happened to brush against Moore, in an exercise of the marathoners' traditionally good manners towards one another. Nothing in the way of a "pardon" or "excuse me" was forthcoming from Cierpinski, however. Shorter did not even know who Cierpinski was. He wore no emblem or colors to identify his nationality. As the race heated up and the adrenaline was running high, Cierpinski's tactic led to pushing and shoving between the two of them.

This annoyance was not the only pressure on Shorter. Lasse Viren from Finland, the preeminent distance runner in the world, who less than twenty-four hours before had won the 10,000-meter and a few days before that the 5,000-meter, decided to enter the marathon. Viren's last mile of the 10,000-meter (6.2 miles) was done in 4:09. There was no one in the world who could match his ability to run one killer quarter after another. Viren had won a total of four Olympic gold medals in two Olympics. He decided to try for a medal in the marathon because Paavo Nurmi, a national legend in Finland, had never done it, and because a gold would give him the "triple crown" of long-distance running. Only Emil Zatopek had achieved that. Of Viren's endurance, it was said that he did 200 kilometers per week, including runs of over 50 kilometers (31.1 miles), but he had never raced a marathon before. He represented a large and troublesome question mark to the other runners, particularly Shorter and Rodgers.

Rodgers, worried about Shorter's and Viren's speed and his own relative lack, decided to push the pace against them from the beginning in an attempt to break them down. Rodgers didn't have to take the lead, however, because others took it, even forty-four-year-old Jack Foster from New Zealand.

Goran Bengtsson of Sweden led the pack through the 5 K point in 15:19, a 4:56 pace; through the 10 K point in 30:48; through the 15 K point (9.3 miles) in 45:58; and through the 20 K point in 1:01:22. Shorter then put on his first surge, which lost Bengtsson. But the pack soon caught up with him, and when they did, Cierpinski surged, as if to say to Shorter, "I can do that too." Shorter and the pack containing Rodgers and Viren made it back to him quickly.

At the 25 K mark Shorter put on his second surge, a big one, and took a lead of about 40 yards. Rodgers seemed to favor his right leg. He had trouble in his forefoot. Only Cierpinski and the Indian Suigh, picked up the pace and followed. Cierpinski made it back to Shorter. Suigh didn't. He wasn't used to running in shoes and his feet were bloody.

Between 25 K and 30 K the battle raged between Shorter and Cierpinski; it became a series of sprint races, with Cierpinski always matching a Shorter surge with one of his own. The 30 K point was passed in 1:32:08. People standing there saw a grim and worried Shorter and a placid Cierpinski.

At about 34 K Cierpinski got away from Shorter and at 35 K he was 13 seconds ahead. At about 39 K he could see the Olympic Stadium ahead and turned to look behind. Shorter was about 200 yards behind. Cierpinski went through the 40 K point in 2:03:12; Shorter in 2:04:34; Karl Lismont in 2:04:36 and Viren in 2:05:34. The race for the medals was over, except between Don Kardong and Lismont. Cierpinski continued to pour it on, nevertheless, finishing with a 65-second lap of the stadium track, in the time of 2:09:55, 50 seconds ahead of Shorter. He then ran his victory lap also in 65 seconds. Shorter waited for him to finish his victory lap and to shake his hand. Don Kardong could not hold off Lismont who outsprinted him to the tape to win the bronze medal by 3 seconds. Lasse Viren finished fifth in 2:13:10, Bill Rodgers limped in to a fortieth place finish in 2:25, and the last to finish, sixtieth was Lucio Guardrella, from Bolivia, in 2:45.

At the awards ceremonies when Cierpinski and Shorter were on their pedestals waiting to receive the medals, the stadium reverberated with a chant started by the thousands of Americans: "Shorter, Shorter, Shorter . . ." He was still a hero to them, and more importantly not a loser to himself. He said that he did not "consider coming in second as losing," and told John Jerome of *Outside* magazine: "I was as ready as I could have been at Montreal. I was really fit. I ran a 2:10. It was just that I got to a certain point in the race and tried to break it open, and I got away from everyone but one guy. He got away from me. I ran about as hard as I could, I just didn't win. That's all. I've never been interested in post-mortems."

In 1975 Shorter was graduated from the University of Florida Law School and while he was training for the 1976 Olympics he was studying for the Colorado bar exam which he passed. He was admitted to practice in Colorado. His wife, whom he married in 1970, came from Boulder; so it was logical that they move there, particularly with the many advantages that it offers. It has mile-high altitude and is close to the University of Colorado with its indoor track and other training facilities. Boulder is not far from the Denver airport from which Shorter does a great deal of traveling. Boulder is an "up" place to live, with its mountain beauty and clean air. It is a mecca for young, out-of-doors people: runners, bicyclers, backpackers and mountain climbers. Shorter began the practice of law there after he was admitted to the bar, but he also tried to keep up a full racing schedule after Montreal. Lawyers unfortunately, live sedentary lives with long hours in an office behind a desk pouring energy into the problems of others. The law is a "jealous mistress" who won't stand other love affairs, and Shorter had one of long standing with running. The practice of law was incompatible with his real love. It would not yield enough time for training and for traveling.

A store to sell running gear would, however, provide a livelihood and allow him the time for training and traveling. His working hours could be tailored to his lifestyle of "stiff, groggy morning, rich, vigorous afternoons and nodding evenings," as Kenny Moore put it. Shorter put a shower in the store even before a cash register, because everyone working there was a runner and used the store as a training base. Soon there were three stores in operation.

On the flight to the New York City Marathon in 1977, Shorter discussed with Jim Lillstrom, who had the seat next to him, his inability to find good running shorts, which were needed for his new store. They decided to make their own and enlisted the help of John Kubiak of Seattle, Washington, who is a runner and a manufacturer of ski wear. The three went into business making shorts, shirts, warmup suits and rain suits. Overnight "Shorter Shorts" became a rage. At a sporting goods trade show in Chicago in the spring of 1978, the three business partners (Lillstrom has the corporate title of "Prince") received, the first day, $10,000 worth of orders for Shorter running gear. In not many months in business, they were deluged with orders to the point that they got three months behind and had to stop taking any more. Today the "Frank Shorter Running Gear" label can be found in just about every sports and department store in the country. The gear is well-designed and well-made with "breathing" and "wicking" fabrics that all runners want.

The 1977 New York City Marathon was the culmination of nearly a year of trouble with Shorter's left ankle. He had to drop out at the 15-mile point on the Manhattan side of the Fifty-Ninth Street Bridge. He had experienced one high point in early 1977, however, and that was running 2 miles in 8:26.2 indoors in the Coliseum in Los Angeles, doing the last half mile in a 1:56, which astonished even himself. The operation on his left ankle took place on April 26, 1978 and it was not until April 28, 1979, a year almost to the day after the operation that he ran well competitively, finishing third in 48:34 behind Craig Virgin and Bill Rodgers in the Trevira 10-miler.

Things were not really working right biomechanically though; the "running machine" was out of sync. His left leg was smaller than the right, weakened by the lack of use following the operation, and the right one strengthened by overcompensation for the left. The right leg then began giving him trouble.

As the 1980 Olympics loomed on the horizon, Shorter was still struggling to get himself straightened out. He had his old Yale coach, Bob Giegengack, out to Boulder to see if he could help him find that seamless fluidity. Giegengack found one minor flaw—Shorter's left shoulder was thrust too far forward.

When Shorter was asked why he would not pick himself to make the Olympic team in 1980, he said in *The Runner* magazine: "If I were running 28 for 10,000, 13:25 for 5,000 or 46 minutes for 10 miles, yes. But I'm not there yet." He also said, after the Trevira 10-miler, "Right now, I'm like I was when I was in high school, just plugging along, trying to run better, watching people run past me and telling myself, O.K., next time I'll be a little closer, and maybe one day I'll be out in front."

In the 1979 Boston Marathon, he had a great deal of trouble with stiffness and finished in seventy-eighth place, 2 seconds slower than the Olympic trials qualifying time of 2:21:54. Two days before he had assisted at the birth of his first child, Kenneth Alexander. In October 1979, he ran a 2:16:16, which qualified him for the trials but left him in "no-man's land," because he was a long way from 2:10, which is what everybody expected it would take to make the team, yet not far enough away to give up trying.

The three runners Shorter picked to make the Olympic team were Bill Rodgers, Jeff Wells, and Tony Sandoval. Rodgers is thought by most people in the free world to be the best today because of his consistency: four consecutive New York City Marathon wins and four Boston Marathon wins, and his great times, particularly the 2:09:27 in the eighty-third annual Boston Marathon in 1979.

Jeff Wells has been coming on strong as a world class marathoner. In 1978 he nearly caught Bill Rodgers at the end of the Boston Marathon. As it happened, a motorcycle policeman advised Rodgers who was in the lead that another runner was catching up with him. Rodgers wouldn't believe him, and began to berate him for trying to push him towards a record. In response, the policeman told Rodgers to turn around and look for himself. There was Jeff Wells, bearing down on him with less than a mile to go. It was a wild spring to the finish line, with Rodgers winning by only about 10 yards. Wells had run the fastest second half of a marathon ever run, 64 minutes. Tony Sandoval just missed the 1976 Olympic team by one place to Don Kardong. Sandoval and Wells had tied for first place in the 1979 Nike Marathon in 2:10:20.

With the Soviet Union's refusal to pull out of Afghanistan, the United States boycott of the 1980 Olympic Summer Games in Moscow became effective. The United States Olympic trials held on the Skylon Marathon course in Buffalo, New York, in May 1980, would serve as the grand finale, although the top three would earn a free trip to Fukuoka.

An unknown, Gary Fanelli, led the field through the halfway point in 1:04:39, where he began to slow with a blister on his foot. Shorter was not in the pack that took up the lead. He had faltered at about 10 miles, plagued by stiffness. At 19 miles Benji Durden surged into the lead followed by Sandoval and Hefner. Durden is known for his training in sweatsuits even in the 100-degree heat of his hometown, Atlanta, Georgia. He says that heat is "just another stress." Between 21 and 22 miles Sandoval ran a 4:44 pace and took the lead and went on to win in 2:10:18. Durden was next in 2:10:40, and Hefner third, in 2:10:54. Shorter finished in 2:23:23 in eighty-fifth place. He said later, as reported in *Running Times*, "I'll back off, I'll do something else for a while. I'll run, but I've got to start over. It's going to be hard. Maybe my time has passed. I tried to maintain my intensity, but I broke down. Go talk to the winner."

The winner of the 1980 Olympic Marathon in Moscow was Waldemar Cierpinski of East Germany in the time of 2:11:03. He is the only man other than Bikila to have won back-to-back Olympic marathons.

Shorter gave up medical school to pursue his running, even when running held out only a vague possibility of an

Olympic medal. He gave up a career in the law for which he had spent three years in school and instead went into business, because business would give him the time to run. He is not a doctor or a lawyer, or even a businessman for that matter. His businesses are run by others. What he is is a runner. He has been accused of running to enhance his business interests. His accusers have it backwards. He has worked things out business-wise so that he can be free to be what he is, a runner; a runner who has led so many others to live more closely to the design of nature.

T.B.

Bill Rodgers

BIRD MAN OF BOSTON

BILL RODGERS runs toward the finish line of the 1978 New York City Marathon. He is out in front but frazzled and tired. Wasted really. Wasted from an early battle for the lead with Gary Bjorklin. Helicopter rotors roar above his head. Wind sweeps up dust in his eyes. The lead car, a Subaru, blows exhaust fumes in his face. Applause surrounds him, harsh, distorted, reverberating with his steps. Breathless, eyes tearing, ears struck and ringing, he begins to look from the inside out, withdrawing, "spacing out," envisioning for an instant that he will fall into an open manhole in the street—falling, drifting, floating, like some kind of Alice in Wonderland of the running world.

Rodgers finished the race. Despite the fatigue and "the

strange fleeting thoughts," he won the race for the third year in a row. Still—I thought later—if he had fallen like Alice, into a strange wonderland, into an urban underworld, his fantasy would probably be to fall straight through and land on the other side of the earth, on the winner's stand, listening to "Oh say can you see . . . and the rockets' red glare," as the winner of the gold medal in the marathon in the 1980 Olympics in Moscow.

With the U.S. boycott of the 1980 Olympics in Moscow, Rodgers's fantasy has been revised in time and place. He is training with the 1984 Olympics in Los Angeles in mind but with politicians lately acting as coaches for amateur athletes and the fate of the modern Olympics uncertain, Rodgers

Bill Rodgers.
(STEVE RONAGHAN)

would rather enjoy his running today and take his races as they come.

Look—and you will see him running on the streets of Boston, jogging through Cleveland Circle and sweating out speed workouts at the tartan track at Boston College. You'll see other runners, too. Pregnant women. Businessmen without their briefcases. College professors without their podiums. Students—trying to remain healthy or sweat out a hangover or release the pressures that school can bring. They run all day in colorful "underwear," dodging Boston's famous reckless drivers and breathing car fumes that constrict their breath. They run at night with gaudy orange-colored running shoes and phosphorescent vests, as trolley cars ignite sparks that light up the bars, Chip's Discotheque and Maryanne's Pub, where students, mostly from Boston College, wait on long lines to get into the crowded bars.

At the heart of all this running is the Bill Rodgers Running Center—a haven for area runners who stop in to buy running clothes, ask running advice and "get into" what is second only to running itself, talking about it. If you don't see him in the streets, you might catch him there. Around eleven o'clock, William Henry Rodgers, one of the world's greatest athletes, will emerge from his tiny basement store and lead the running parade.

Ever since his underdog victory in the 1975 Boston Marathon, Rodgers has become a king-of-the-road personage, a Pied Piper figure in Boston. Yet becoming the greatest has not made him any less gracious. Curiously frail and lean, gentle and resolute, Rodgers still runs through the streets of the various communities in Boston, inviting people to run along with him and wishing luck to those who wish it for him.

He signs autographs. He answers all letters. His intelligent, guileless candor with reporters is renowned. He is as friendly and convivial a celebrity as any sixteen-year-old could dream of meeting.

Training now, along the icy chop of the Charles River, his hair flapping, his body at full sail—wet, tremulous and taut —one can imagine him thinking, wandering back through memory with the speed of dreams, to Patriots Day and the running of the Boston Marathon.

He remembers standing on the sidewalk, watching the crowding bodies pass him and thinking, "I'll never run one of those crazy things." Some years hence he led the crazed and often unattractive display towards the finish line at the Prudential Center in Boston.

He ran in blue jean cutoffs, white workingman's gloves and a T-shirt with "Boston GBTC" (Greater Boston Track Club) in handwritten letters. The crowd overflowed from the sidewalks, narrowing the roadway and at times clogging it, as runners tried to pass and people were pushed and stepped on in the backwash.

Rodgers ran up the middle of the crowd, moving as smoothly as a scull through the Charles River. Each mile passing, passing, in less than 5 minutes per mile; the neighborhood crowd mad with encouragement and approval. The miles getting more difficult now, the noise keeping him going when he felt like quitting.

His speed was intense. Many high school runners can't break 5 minutes for one mile. Rodgers ran 4:58 per mile for 26.2 miles: 4:58 per mile despite stopping four times; once to tie his shoe and three times to get a drink of water. When asked why he stopped, he said, "I just can't hold the cup while I'm running."

At the end, with race watchers joining in a resounding din that seemed to shake the panes of glass in the Hancock Building beyond, Rodgers crossed the finish line with a time of 2:09:55, surpassing Frank Shorter's American record by 30 seconds and establishing himself as one of the fastest marathon runners in the world.

As a boy growing up in Newington, Connecticut, Rodgers loved to chase butterflies. He collected them, put them in cases and hung them on the walls. Blue butterflies in early spring, the Spicebush and the Eastern Tiger Swallowtails in summer, and of course, in the fall, winging southward, the monarch.

He had other hobbies, too. Hobbies that kept him moving, kept him fit. "I was in the Boy Scouts. We hiked and did some hunting and fishing and camping. Sometimes I played baseball, touch football. We'd walk 5 miles to go fishing. I was more active in some ways. Moving a lot."

In high school Rodgers ran on the track team, chasing competitors. When he first started, "9 minutes around the block was a long training run." He says he was a "mediocre" runner then. His high school coach once told his mother, in effect, "I wouldn't get too excited about his prospects."

Rodgers kept a running diary then, in a small, spiral note book.

Oct. 6, 1963
Ran 5½ laps
around the block
about 2¾ miles,
very tired.

Oct. 7, 1963
Ran 1 mile and 3/10ths
for gym. Strong

sprint, solid first.
Did about 2.3 miles
for Cross Country. 6
50 yd. windsprints.

Oct. 8, 1963
Ran 1 3/10ths for
Cross Country. Did
6:16; fairly good.*

In his sophomore year, at age fifteen-and-a-half, the young running diarist won a 2 1/2-mile cross-country race. Running was "half exploration and adventure" then. "I loved running in high school. It was new. I was good at it."

Track practice was then similar to other sports: Calisthenics, hard sprint workouts, coaches controlling everything. On occasion Bill and his brother Charlie would go out for long runs with the other eight members of the track team. Rodgers was always out in front of everyone during training sessions. "Bill would always go down all the side streets," his brother Charlie said, "as the rest of us took the short cuts."

Rodgers started running over 5 miles just for the fun of it. The longest event in high school was the 2-mile. He went to the New England Cross-Country Championships his last two years. Yet it was the really long runs that Rodgers liked.

One day, feeling especially fired and fit, he ran 5 miles up Route 66 in Connecticut—10 miles all together. Back then, for a high school runner, that was an amazing statistic that sped through the hallways of Newington High School.

Rodgers started college in time of rebellion, of protest, of earnest outrage against the Vietnam war. It was 1967—Wesleyan University, Wesleyan Connecticut. Long, roguish hair

* Printed in *The Runner* magazine.

was the norm. Rodgers wore his hair at shoulder length, some-times in a ponytail. He wore faded pastel blue jeans. He smoked marijuana. "I never really got into drugs," he says, however, "it wasn't good for me psychologically." He was, in short, what most college kids were considered in those days, a hippie.

The contentious atmosphere on campus was not exactly right for the making of American records. Regimentation and discipline, the kind that it takes to make a great runner, were suspect values associated with parents, college presidents and, worse, the military.

The war had turned people inward, too. Students concerned with peace were also looking for "good times," for self-discovery and, as the war "deescalated" and the 1960s ended, for escape.

It was in this self-absorbed atmosphere in America that jogging became suddenly popular. At the same time Bill Rodgers began the long-distance running that would make him the greatest runner, the most elusive fugitive, in America.

Rodgers was fortunate to meet people who preferred long, slow, road running to grueling, monotonous track work-outs. He met a tall, thin wire brush of a distance runner named Ambrose Burfoot. Burfoot liked to run in the woods and parks and around the lakes in rural Connecticut. The kid chasing butterflies always loved the woods. The adult hadn't changed. In a published biography, Rodgers described his connections with the outdoors. "One of the most important things about running is the relationship of man and woman to earth and nature. I think it is at the heart of why so many people are running. It is as simple as that. There is a little Thoreau in all of us.

"As we become increasingly involved in technology, science, and business, we should not lose that instinct, that feeling for the earth. Running is a very beautiful way to bring out those healthy feelings."

Rodgers followed Burfoot. The Connecticut landscape, always shifting, provided constant entertainment. Burfoot was serious, self-motivated. Rodgers, normally under the tutelage of a coach, was neither. Burfoot says he is always asked whether he knew then that Rodgers would become the runner he is today. "No," he answers, "I didn't know. I knew he had talent." He was always surprised at the ease with which he ran, how he just floated along in his shadow. "But you could never predict," he says.

Running never became serious in college. Rodgers thought that there were more important things to worry about. He joined the antiwar movement. He supported the student strike in 1970 and applied for conscientious objector draft status.

Throughout his senior year these larger issues preoccupied Rodgers. He waited for C.O. classification. His high school coach refused to support his conscientious objector claims. Finally, he was given alternative service wheeling patients and dead bodies through the hallways of Peter Bent Brigham Hospital in Boston.

Rodgers was then smoking a pack of cigarettes a day—Winstons and Larks usually. He wasn't running. He hadn't run in over two years. He was in a "dead-end boring job," living in a tenement, collecting food stamps. There was only one good thing happening: he met his future wife Ellen in a bar in Boston.

Rodgers doesn't recall the exact reasons that he started running again. Getting fired from his job was part of it.

Losing his motorcycle was, too. He started at the YMCA track and within a year he was up to 100 miles a week. His new girl friend and future wife wasn't sure how to take it. She told *Runners World* magazine, "I thought 'What is this? He wants to go running more than he wants to see me?' I eventually changed my perspective on his priorities," she said. He ran his first marathon in Boston in 1974 but heated up too fast and dropped out at 20 miles. He quit running for two months; he tried "to analyze" why he bombed out.

But 1975 was different. He worked at the Fernald School in Belmont, Massachusetts—a state institution for the retarded, and studied for his master's in special education at Boston College. He found his work at the school satisfying. (He later taught emotionally disturbed children for two years.) His running proved more fulfilling, too. He made the American team for the World Cross-Country Championships in Morocco, and came in third in a field of international runners. Rodgers knew where he was headed now. That spring he won the Boston Marathon.

Rodgers's rise to the pinnacle of American road racing paralleled the rise of the sport itself. The latter is a story of health and fashion, the former a story of one man's dominance in a sport where numerous and often unknown circumstances seem to conspire to defeat anyone.

Rodgers has had his problems. Problems with heat and jet lag and running too fast, too soon. With heat mostly. He hates the heat. It is the principal reason for many of his defeats.

In the 1976 Montreal Olympics, his temperature stayed down, but a foot injury prevented any chance of winning there. Yet, he still ran hard for the first 13 miles, ran "suicidal" so that Lasse Viren, the favorite, would not win without a struggle. He finished fortieth. Since then, his injuries have been minor; his luck in this regard, he freely admits, has been major, and his control of the lead in American road racing has been without relent.

He's won the "prestigious" Boston Marathon three times; the New York City Marathon, the "people's marathon," four years in succession. He's run faster than any Amercian in four different marathons. He holds five other national records and a world record of 1:14:11.8 in the 25 kilometer run. His consistently fast times could not be matched by anyone—not even Derek Clayton—the Australian who holds the world record of 2:08:34 in the marathon.

In 1978, in distances varying from 10 kilometers to the marathon, Rodgers won twenty-eight consecutive races. More accurately, he nearly swept the streets clean of competition. It was all becoming routine. People just presumed Rodgers would win. That is, until the end of the 1978 Boston Marathon.

Frank Shorter set a pace that Rodgers thought was very fast. It was a fairly good day for running: 46 degrees and no sun. Still, it was too fast. Shorter spurted ahead about 200 yards. Rodgers went right after him; he couldn't let him get too far ahead. Too dangerous. Shorter then in the reachable distance; Rodgers spurting, running up next to Shorter. Then the others filling the gap, with all the front runners soon in confluence.

The start had been smooth, the great mass of six thousand runners disassembling without too many stepped-on heels or elbowed ribs. In the first adrenaline-fueled mile, Rodgers passed Jerome Drayden and Don Kardong of Canada. Then he passed Jeff Wells of Texas, feeling good. Wells said hello—Rodgers would later wish he had said goodbye.

By Natick, about 10 miles into the race, Shorter dropped behind. "I noticed Shorter was breathing hard," Rodgers said. "And I thought 'O.K. that takes care of Frank.' " Kevin Ryan of New Zealand and Rodgers were engaged in leg-to-leg combat with Essa Tikkanen of Finland laying back watching the conflict. Ryan ran ahead. Rodgers followed. Ryan ahead again. Rodgers shadowing. Tikkanen behind, the detached observer, waited for either to weaken.

When they hit the dreaded hill in Newton, "Heartbreak Hill," Rodgers heaved and pumped his way out in front, breaking the record for the 4 miles by 21 seconds. The record was Boston's oldest time record, set back in 1965 by Morio Shigematsu.

On the downside of the great heartbreaker, past Boston College, Rodgers's legs weakened. His calves buckled. He was hurting.

Rodgers described his pain to his friend Amby Burfoot in an interview in *Runners World* magazine. "This is the brutal point of the marathon, you know—where you really start to cave in. So that's when I started slowing down. Just trying to maintain.

"The thing was I couldn't see anybody behind me."

Jeff Wells, a divinity student from the Dallas Theological Seminary, decided about halfway that he felt good and that he wasn't working hard enough. "All of a sudden it hit me; I hadn't given 100 percent as I had promised the Lord. It was then and there I knew I had to kick it for him."

With Wells kicking for the Lord, setting a record for the distance from Wellesley College to the finish (1:04:22), Rodgers, still, was unaware of him.

Rodgers asked a motorcycle cop how much of a lead he

had. "About a minute," he answered. Then 2 minutes later, he added: "There's someone moving up fast."

Rodgers was furious at the cop. He thought his answer was just a trick to get him to move faster. Then the cop said, "Turn around. You can see him there."

Sure enough, Wells was there, running with fervor, closer now, stalking Bill Rodgers like he was after the devil himself, with Rodgers, weakened and despairing, looking for a distant finish line to save him.

"I started thinking," Rodgers said, "if only there was 26 miles instead of 26 miles 385 yards. In my mind I was looking at tomorrow's headlines and getting a horrible feeling because the headline had said I finished second."

Wells gained on him steadily, presumably asking for more speed. Distance was running out. Rodgers's legs hardened like molten rock. The sight of the onrushing Wells was "the ultimate nightmare."

You've probably had the nightmare. You're running from something; running with legs swollen and heavy, like you're in deep soft sand and an undertow is sucking you away from shore. You're not sure what it is that's chasing you. It's a murderous, undefined thing. It moves closer. You try to free your legs, speed them up. It's no use. Frantic, thrashing, you struggle forward but everything is too heavy. It's suddenly upon you and you surface violently from sleep.

Rodgers, faltering but still fleet, took the last corner, thinking he "was on two wheels." Wells ran into a motorcycle cop but sidestepped his way past him. Rodgers looked back again and Wells was right behind him: a realization of that recurring familiar nightmare. And then, and then, only strides before the tape, Rodgers knew he had won. He threw himself into the finish line, relieved that he was safe, that the nightmare was over.

It was one of the closest finishes in marathon history and "the most painful finish" of Rodgers's career.

The following year, a week before the race, Rodgers dreamed that he was stuck wearing his training shoes at the starting line: stuck at the back of the pack. He often dreams before the Boston Marathon—sometimes as many as three times—dreams of running up a hill slowly with people passing him. Once in a confused, twisted nightmare, he had to run through cubicles to get to the finish.

This year the nightmare would only occur in his sleep. On a cold, overcast day, 50 yards from the finish, Rodgers clearly saw the finish line clock reading 2:09:32. He was the leader. No one was in sight behind him. He pressed for British runner Ron Hill's best time of 2:09:28. He finished with the clock reading 2:09:27.

It was a new American record, just 53 seconds off Derek Clayton's world record and the fourth fastest marathon ever run. It was run against what was perhaps the finest group of marathoners ever to gather for one race. On the winner's stand, open-mouthed, with the green victory wreath over his head, (the crown of thorns as Rodgers calls it), and his Snoopy hat faithfully at his side, Rodgers thrust his gloved fist up in triumph to the crowd.

Unlike athletes in other sports who relax in the off-season, playing golf, gaining weight and enjoying their luxuriant salaries, Rodgers is always in training. Since 1973, he has been averaging 130 miles a week, with weeks of over 200 miles covered. That averages to over 18 miles a day, every day, for seven years.

To the nonathlete the compilation of miles is inconceivable. To the partially athletic, it is a physical feat that in itself merits honor and glory. To the athlete, say someone who has run a marathon, the reaction to such mileage is an exasperating question: how do they do it?

The stress is tremendous. In addition to long slow miles —what is called LSO (long slow distance)—run at about 6:50 per mile pace, Rodgers does speed workouts. (A 6:50 pace cannot be called slow by common standards but when you consider miles in a marathon run at a 4:48 pace, it's understandable that Rodgers 6:50 would be comfortable enough for him to breathe normally.)

Once a week, after running 11 miles in the morning, Rodgers will begin his afternoon workout with a 68-second quarter mile at the track at Boston College. He'll then jog 200 meters, run a half mile at a 68-second pace and jog another 200 meters. Finishing the set, he'll run three-quarters of a mile at the same pace. After repeating this routine three times, he is done. Occasionally, to enliven the endless circling, circling, he will vary the combinations, running mile intervals at a pace of 4:45—six times.

The numbers may not tell of the work here; work that is mentally and physically exhausting. The explanation itself is overworked. Words seem weak in describing the training of a world class marathon runner. Few athletes in preparation for any sport go through such unremitting stress. Runners like Rodgers are tough beyond our use of the word in sports: a toughness not of the quick, violent act, but of work and patience and endurance over time, something that daily tries a person's resolve and develops a gritty tenacity in mind and body.

Rodgers never lets up. Even when he is traveling he will run through airports, filling up idle time, fulfilling his mileage quota.

Sometimes the stress is counterproductive. Over 100 miles a week, old injuries that never really healed partially return. Sprained ankles. Twisted knees. Back problems. Runners know the feelings. At night you often twitch in sleep. Your heart races. You sweat. Not sure of where you are, frantic for perspective, you glance quickly from side to side. In the morning you awaken so stiff you wonder whether you moved at all during the night. Your pulse is fast. You're shaky and strung out. You move from your bed like a seedy drunk who's just been told he can't sleep on the park bench anymore.

Rodgers has named this "overuse syndrome." There are symptoms. He gets colds, loses his balance, stumbles on curbs. The prescription for the condition is sleep. Rodgers sleeps nine to ten hours a night. Like most people, he would like more.

When Rodgers thinks he is seriously tired or slightly injured—about six times a year—he stays in bed all day, idling, reading, but mostly sleeping.

The following day, he is "zippy"—Rogers's seemingly favorite word for feeling good. He'll run 11 miles hard in the morning and around 5 o'clock, to complete the second part of the daily ritual, he'll run another 10 miles. The cycle will begin again: a rhythm of stress, recovery and strength.

"Some days I feel I'm flipping out, out there," Rodgers says. He's been known to swear softly to himself and bang mailboxes along the route that circles back to his return address.

Rodgers's running style is singular in the length of time

he spends in the air. Rodgers's friends say he is airborne half of the time. Most pictures of Rodgers running show him aloft, both legs outstretched, feet pointed, floating.

The bird analogies are obvious, striking. Bill Rodgers is a reincarnated American eagle. In marathons the connections with a prehistoric pterodactyl and its menacing 6-foot wing span, are conspicuous. He is a bird-man—of Boston. His nose is long, narrow—beakish. His 5'8", 128-pound body is only 7 percent fat. (At that weight, birdlike, his bones might even be hollow.) His appearance at a lectern while speaking publicly reminds one of those delicate white creatures seen in bays and marshes—egrets and the like—still and pensive at first sighting but always prepared to flap and vanish at the slightest provocation.

He is also a deadly downhill runner. In the 1979 Boston Marathon, using the momentum provided by the last 6 miles of the downhill, he wheeled past Seiko of Japan at the 18-mile mark for his third Boston victory and a new American record of 2:09:27.

After his record-breaking marathon, Rodgers was sore for three weeks. After the third or fourth day the fatigue declined. It usually takes him three or four weeks to recover fully.

Slowly, improving daily, he gets back to feeling good. The season will then determine his training and racing schedule. In the winter he runs long and slow—140 to 170 miles a week—through the cold and often snowy streets of Boston. Lately, he has taken trips to California and Arizona to run in the sun during the really frigid months. He is usually training hard for the Boston Marathon in the spring. In the summer, he takes it easy. His light skin and fair hair, he says, make him genetically unprepared for the heat. Fall is the time he says that he is ready to race.

Well, it was fall in New York, 1979. Because of his losses the past summer, especially the Montreal International Marathon, Rodgers really wanted to win. Wanted to win, too, because of what had started in the New York media and was now rumored in the running community: Rodgers in a slump, Shorter on the rise.

Rodgers prepared for the race with a routine that has worked for him. His training progressively declines up to the day of the race. The respite begins after a hard week of workouts. For a Sunday race, starting on Wednesday, his mileage in double workouts will go from 23 to 18 on Wednesday, 14 on Thursday and 6 on Friday. Saturday he will jog 3 miles, trying to remain loose. He is concerned with getting a lot of rest, watching his diet and not injuring himself.

The night before a marathon he is tense. The media pressures are immense. The layoff gives him excess energy. He sleeps "fitfully."

Sunday, October 22, he awakened two hours before the race. It was predicted to be a hot Indian summer day but cool then, with fog and low steel-wool clouds drawing towards the southeast.

He ate a light breakfast of regular coffee and buttered toast. "No pancakes," he says. "I like to feel light." (Rodgers is known for his love of junk food. He eats a lot of sugar, cheeseburgers, cold pizza. Sometimes he gets up during the night and eats a fourth meal, spooning his beloved mayonnaise out of a jar.) That day, in the remaining two hours, he drank a quart of liquid. Dehydration can be a problem for him. He sipped right up to the start of the race. He jogged, stretching out his muscles, picking up speed at times to loosen his body. He wanted to be warm when the starting cannon fired.

The race began when a pack of runners fired out from the start 6 seconds before the cannon. Rodgers held fast with a few other stalwarts, as a party of physicians, lawyers, bureaucrats, bums and other assorted renegades jostled and shoved and rushed past him.

The cannon finally went off and Rodgers experienced what it is like for the ruck—the majority of the 11,533 starters: you are part of the herd, viciously protective of your own territory and looking to get ahead once survival is assured.

The overanxious starters caused a near-disaster. Police motorcycles, media trucks and buses were inundated by the flash flood of runners and lay adrift in the rapids like overturned boats.

Frank Shorter, among others, was squeezed between two trucks, then honked off the road by the press van trying to pilot its way out of trouble.

Here, at the mile mark, Rodgers waded in one-hundred-fiftieth place. "I had to do a bit of zigzagging," he said.

About the beginning of races Rodgers says, "I'm very confident at the start. I have a tremendous amount of composure." He thinks to himself: "I want to save my energy. I want to save my energy."

Rodgers expected the skies to clear and the sun to come out when it was least appreciated—at the end of the race—so he paced himself for a hot finish.

Unbeknownst to Rodgers, Kirk Pfeiffer, a twenty-three-year-old graduate of the University of Colorado, was running at a course record pace. By the Queensboro Bridge, about 18 miles into the marathon, he had a minute and a half lead.

Rodgers, running with Steve Kenyon from England, moved through the frontrunners stride by stride, mentally checking each off as he ran. "He [Kenyon] knew many of the European guys so he could identify them for me," Rodgers said. "He'd point and say 'that's so and so,' and he'd tell me what he's done in races, then we'd pick them off one at a time."

Rodgers has what he calls "a sense of the marathon." He has "specialized in the marathon and has learned it well." It's helped him remain consistent. "I'm still learning," he says, however, "I've run twenty-five marathons. That helps me some. I pick my races carefully. I'm very observant. You have to be able to sense the pace, sense your body and the fatigue you're developing. When you feel it really early in the race, using your mind to fight your body doesn't really work. You can't maintain.

"Another thing is it is always safe to follow in a marathon. You save a certain amount of energy by running behind someone. They're blocking the wind. Psychologically, it's important. You're being pulled by him. It's much easier physically and psychologically. With about 5 miles left, you go. You have to devise strategies to goof them up. You use your state of mind and experience to your advantage."

Rodgers showed good marathon sense. His patient, deliberate approach continued for most of the race; through Brooklyn, through Bedford-Stuyvesant. He ran on steamy, potholed streets. Uneven streets. Streets with sewers and manhole covers and steel gratings. Now in Williamsburg, now in Greenpoint, he passed the devout Hasidic Jews with their austere black dress, passed the Polish neighborhoods near the halfway point, as kids looked up at him as if at the towering buildings, and the Polish people present greeted him with enthusiasm otherwise reserved for their Pope in visitation.

Rodgers's tactics worked. The afternoon sun reflected through the steamy haze, striking the now-vulnerable runners. At length, Rodgers could make out the weakening figure of Kirk Pfeiffer. "When I saw him," Rodgers said, "I knew he was tired." Pfeiffer had hit the wall.

In distance running the wall goes up when the body's available sugar runs out and a switchover is made to sugar, called glycogen, in the muscles. The effect is similar to trying to get out of bed in the morning when you haven't had enough sleep that night. Time springs ahead. You're suddenly struck with the feeling of what it's like to be old and arthritic. Muscles stiffen. Breathing labors. Running becomes more like scuba diving: you run through thick air with heavy legs. Breathing is exaggerated. The blurred crowd's clapping is muffled but still resonant, like the sound of a boat engine under water.

In its advanced stages, dementia sets in. You space out. Froth at the mouth. You might even find yourself—as actor

Bill Rodgers finishing the New York City Marathon. (STEVE RONAGHAN)

Bruce Dern did at the end of a 60-mile run—thinking you're still running when you've stopped a long while ago.

Since fatigue while running, as well as in other pursuits, can be largely psychological, "the wall" can be erected to towering proportions or mentally bulldozed to tumbling bricks. I get to be an expert bricklayer at the end of the marathon, building a wall of China, building a line of defense that would stop a Pittsburgh Steeler. Pfeiffer, however, seemed to be legitimately out of sugar.

At 23.2 miles up into the hills, and the hellish colors of Central Park in fall, Rodgers passed Pfeiffer. Rodgers, ever congenial, said, "Hi Kirk," then left him in the street dirt. Pfeiffer near a 6-minute pace, "gutting it out," holding on to second place. Rodgers right on schedule; his right arm bouncing back and forth, back and forth, like a metronome keeping time, as the crowd applauded his precision and he hurled himself into the yellow finish tape all ashen face and hammering head and throbbing heart.

I spoke with Rodgers a few months after the New York race. We sat in an office in the back of his basement store, the Bill Rodgers Running Center in Brighton, Massachusetts. The office, (not his, he says) was also part locker room. There was no attempt to make distinctions between business and running. Here, there are none; they are two legs of the same body. Gym bag next to briefcase. Day-old sweat sock, half-alive on accounting sheet. Why not?

Rodgers is relaxed in this environment. He tipped back in his swivel chair, his splintery legs crossed, his hair still wet from the first of the two runs and showers of the day. It was 12 o'clock. He listened to my questions—concentrating—blinking, and nodding occasionally, as the words connected.

Then his answers would rush out, candid, unself-conscious, surprising himself at times to laughter and always, curiously, revealing what seems to be the two sides to his renowed character.

It's funny. No one seems to be able to explain this apparent split. In the frequent seminars that he gives throughout the northeast, his attitude towards running seems casual. His friend Amby Burfoot says, "In a lot of ways, Bill is still like a thirteen-year-old discovering the joys of running." His attitude is so casual that you wonder how he is able to consistently train hard—how he becomes so tough in marathons. Rodgers says half-seriously, "I'm a Dr. Jekyll and Mr. Hyde." I laughed at his comment. But the joke does well in describing the central paradox of Bill Rodgers's personality: he is a lion and a lamb, a sparrow and a pterodactyl, a gentle man and a ferocious competitor.

Amby Burfoot says he's "never been able to figure it out." He's come up with some outlandish theories, however. One is that Rodgers, very passive normally, lets his aggressive tendencies out on the road. "Most of us have learned to be assertive over the years," he says; Rodgers "hasn't been able to master the idea of saying no." Hence, the "pent-up anger," "killer crush attitude," on the road.

Not a bad explanation. But it confuses me, as I'm sure it does his competitors, that this nice guy is always, always finishing first.

Rodgers has another side, too, a side not explained by Burfoot's theories: he is an outspoken radical. My first question to him was about the bonanza of reporters with their cameras pointed like bazookas at the finish line of the New York City Marathon. Finish line director Dave Pearlman had to rescue Rodgers from the assault. "The New York press are wolves," he said, softly. About his recent losses. ("They were very critical that I wasn't winning every race.") About their coverage of the gold medal–winning Frank Shorter and Bill Rodgers rivalry. ("To the New York media gold medals instantly confer immortality.")

He is critical of the Amateur Athletic Union and the "hypocritical amateur system." He is critical of large corporations who sponsor races in order to cash in on running's popularity, and the obvious corollary—on Bill Rodgers's and other great runners' appeal. He resents corporate race promoters who think that he is going to be their servant. He is critical, finally, of the United States government's decision to boycott the 1980 Olympics in Moscow.

"I'm against political, social, or religious concerns being injected into the Olympic Games," he says. "The Olympic Games are for athletes and I believe athletes should not be used as political 'tools' or 'weapons' of any state or organization. It is particularly reprehensible and unfortunate that the United States has decided to use its athletes in this way in light of the fact that for years our sportswriters and others in our society have maintained our system is a superior sports system due to the fact that there is no government involvement in amateur sport. I guess the truth is evident and speaks for itself. Most shocking of the recent developments has been the sell out by our USOC (United States Olympic Committee) and NCAA (National Collegiate Athletic Association) and other sports organizations that purport to help our athletes. I see positive results of these developments with the speeding up of the elimination of the hypocritical amateur system. With no Olympics to aim for, amateur athletes must ask themselves why they should remain amateur."

The ferocity of his remarks don't seem to fit this gentle

man. I can't imagine him insulting *any* individual. But his determination to have individuals justly treated by institutions has kept him off the Wheaties boxes and out of the fair-haired, all-American athlete role. He is exemplary, however, in every way. He is an athlete with not only two of the fastest, most enduring legs in running history, but an athlete with what is less common, a bright mind, a sympathetic heart.

Rodgers would like to win a gold medal. "I look at it as a goal," he says. "The most respectable goal. The highest single achievement any athlete can get. Just to make an Olympic team is a real honor. If I could get an Olympic medal, my career would be complete."

But his career goals are in perspective. He knows he has to train hard continually and although his Olympic hopes in 1980 were dashed by the Olympic boycott, "I'm aiming for the 1984 Olympics too," he says. "I would like to run as a master, (a category of runners over forty years of age), if there are other good, competitors running . . . I hope to run for the rest of my life."

In his almost comic, earnest but flippant manner, he tells me what he feels sometimes about the Olympics and what I'm sure applies for every race this puzzling man plans to run. "I have this terrible feeling that gnaws in the back of my mind —I'm going to lose! . . . But if I don't make it, I'm sure I'll really enjoy watching it on TV."

R.M.

Walter Stack

STILL DOING THE TURKEY TROT

WALTER STACK sits warily in his simple apartment. His powerful legs are crossed. His slate blue eyes are striking, attentive. He doesn't know what to make of these two skinny whippersnappers who have come to interview him—who are watching him now. So he sits warily and waits.

Moments ago, my co-author and now co-climber and I, begin to descend a hill the size of which we usually only chance while skiing. Stack's apartment is perched on one of seven huge hills in San Francisco; the hill slants down to the Golden Gate Bridge and the fogged-in city below. We ease our Chevy station wagon with its worn brakes and busted valve over the crest of Stack's hill. About 6 miles above San Francisco Bay we start rolling. Paranoid, frantic, my co-climber hits the horn and pumps the brakes and we jerk back and forth, back and forth, with the horn blowing and the valve tapping and the brakes just barely holding on the hill. We park—our wheels turned into the curb to prevent our wonder wagon from rolling into the bay while we're gone.

Up seventy-two steps. Stack shies from our questions, repeating answers he's given before. Nervously, we try to get the conversation moving but Stack just sits, arms folded and nods. At last, he lets go with a tight grin. The jolly, fun-loving Stack is about to loosen up this stiff, cramped-up meeting. "You must be English," Stack says to my co-author. "No," he says. "Irish." I'm laughing. I know it's my friend's formal style of speaking Stack is making fun of. Stack then tells a few bawdy jokes to limber things up some more and finally, modestly, he asks what he's wanted to know from the beginning: "Why am I being interviewed for a book of great marathon runners," he says. "I'm just a turkey; my wife says this isn't the year of the ram. It's the year of the turkey: That's what I am. I'm just a turkey."

There are as many meanings for the expression "turkey" as there are feathers on that awkward, trotting bird. The name usually refers to someone who is also commonly called a "nerd." Nerds are always stumbling over their two large feet, always saying something that is dim-witted and inappropriate. Here, "turkey" is an expression for the nonserious runner who is probably just looking to finish the race. Running "turkeys" are sometimes overweight, generally undertrained and, at the end of a marathon, in trouble.

Stack isn't a turkey. I remember first seeing him at the end of the New York City Marathon. He wasn't exactly gobbling although he could have been if he chose to. He was drinking a can of beer, waving, smiling, leading a group of turkeys who were gasping. Stack says he's "always tired at the end of a marathon."

It's not surprising, really. People who avoid unnecessary movement would be more comfortable staying away from Walter Stack. His limitless energy spreads like laughter. His personality has the effect of a morning shower that suddenly turns cold: He startles, invigorates, makes you move.

Since Stack started running at the age of fifty-eight he has provided evidence that you can be healthy and strong at any age. At age seventy-one he has run over 34,000 miles; miles equivalent to running around the earth nearly one and a half times. He has raced throughout that time simply to participate, but in his participation he has broken records, provided hope for aging athletes and helped change people's perception of old age. His racing record makes a person shake his head and whistle softly in astonishment. Nine 50-milers. Eighty-nine marathons of the 26.2-mile variety. Two 100-milers—a distance from, say, New York to Philadelphia. Stack is, as Dr. Kenneth Cooper's Institute for Aerobic Research wrote of him, "one of the champion athletes in this country of men seventy years of age."

Stack's favorite is the Pikes Peak Marathon. Held in the summer in Manitou Springs, the course rising from 6,500 to 14,110 feet, it is considered the toughest in the country. Stack has run it eleven years in a row. He encourages all runners to try it. The race according to Stack is "the Wimbledon, World Series, and Super Bowl of running."

The ascent is often treacherous. Runners line up heel to toe in places, stepping through narrow rocky aisles. The footing can be dangerous. Higher up, the air is thin and a hindering wind often picks up. Many runners browbeaten by the climb walk the descent.

In his first attempt, Stack ran up, then down, in record time for men sixty to sixty-nine. Before the race Stack wanted to familiarize himself with the course. He wasn't used to the rocky terrain or the altitude. In the nine days prior to the race, he ran the course seven times.

Stack is a rare specimen or better still—a rare bird. Throughout his life, he has been an orphan, a hobo, a soldier, a sailor, a construction worker, a communist, an athlete, and a running enthusiast of the highest quality. He is a funny, earthy character. Always joking. Always checking to see if he's making you laugh.

His speech is renowned in the running community as somewhat "salty." Of his language, Stack once said in an article in *Runners World* magazine, "It's just like my personality. I may appear abrasive to some and may appear shocking to others, but on the other hand, a great many people are pleased by me, identify with me and think I'm colorful. But my general attitude is if anybody doesn't like my personality, it's too late for me to change it. That doesn't mean I'm insensitive. If I see someone who frowns or looks like they're about to frown when I'm talking—especially a woman—and I'm using any of those seven words up for litigation before the Supreme Court, I'll restrain myself."

Stack's looks are startling. Photographs of him dull the youthfulness in his features. His blue eyes are brilliant. His face is angular, handsome. At seventy-one he looks a healthy fifty. You don't believe what you're seeing at first. You'd like to check his birth records to see if he's really over seventy.

Stack is a latter-day Ponce de Leon—the fifteenth century Spanish explorer whose search for the fountain of youth proved futile. Stack hasn't found the fountain of youth, but he seems to have come close to his own source.

"I feel better now than I did twenty years ago," he says. "It is only when I look in the mirror," as he lifts and rubs his chin in the reflection in front of him, "that I say to myself: 'you're getting old.' "

The prolonged youth came unexpectedly. As biographer Bob Bishop explained, "Stack and others like him who previously had exercised to add more life to their years, now began to realize that they might also be adding more years to their lives."

Stack's body is brown and thin with weathered tattoos

Walter Stack.
(TOM LANDECKER)

covering his arms and shoulders. Only his gray, balding head is an index of his age but it is hardly noticeable with his bright eyes, his vast, ironic smile and his legs. The legs. They are sculptured bronze tarnished and tough: young, rocklike monuments to endurance and health. Stack blushes when we compliment them.

Runners are leg conscious. At the starting line of many races, where people's attention might be random, the focus is on legs—lean legs. Runners can usually tell what kind of shape a person is in by looking at the conformation of the calves, the thinness of the thighs. Frank Shorter, an Olympic gold and bronze medalist in the marathon, often checks the competition's legs to see what he is up against. Stack says sometimes women appreciate his legs and tell him so, but "he never really thought about it much."

At the San Francisco Vital Fitness Testing Center, Stack's legs caused quite a stir. Stack once sat down at a hydraulic leg press machine there to see what his "iron man" legs were made of. He started pressing as white-coated technicians with their clipboards marked his progress. Twenty repetitions. Forty repetitions. At fifty repetitions, the point where world class marathoners stop, they started calling in the medical personnel in the area, to witness his phenomenal endurance. Stack was still pumping, as if the machine was broken. At sixty-five repetitions, he stopped. His lungs burned and hissed, his legs shook from the strain. The white coats were amazed. No one of either sex or any age had ever pressed that many before.

Stack doesn't seem to realize the magnitude of what he's accomplished, of what he does every day. For fourteen years he has been bicycling, running and swimming; bicycling, running and swimming, one day after the other, all the while leaving an impressive list of marathons and athletic achievements behind.

Just last year he retired from his job as a hod carrier on a construction site. A hod carrier assists a bricklayer or a mason by carrying his cement and mortar around on a long-handled wooden trough. While he was working, Stack would rise at 2:30 A.M. to complete his play before work: A 5-mile bike ride to the Dolphin Swim Club—an old San Francisco area club of which he is an esteemed member. A 17-mile run across the Golden Gate Bridge, into Sausalito and back. A half-hour swim in the icy water of San Francisco Bay, (49 degrees in winter; up to 59 degrees in summer). And finally, a half-hour melting period at the sauna at the Dolphin Club. Some play.

All of this before a full day of hauling 100-160 pounds of cement around a construction site. Stack arrives home tired. He drinks a couple of bourbon and cokes with his lovely wife Marcie, eats some meat and potatoes and on occasion goes down the mountain to the donut shop and devours a half a dozen donuts. Around 9 or 10 o'clock Stack is ready for his five-and-a-half hours sleep. He doesn't take sleeping pills.

Stack was born poor. In the same way that other young people are shaped by religion or chauvinistic love of country, Stack was indoctrinated by poverty. It explains his idealism and his lifetime participation in leftist politics. He was born in Detroit of Polish parents. At seven, Walt's parents were separated and both Walt and his brother were placed in a number of foster homes and orphanages, one after the other.

Stack had problems in the orphanages. His treatment was often inhumane. He ran away from many of them. When his father died in a bicycle accident, Stack was sent to the Henry

Ford Trade School but soon tired of the monotonous work and ran away again. For the next four to five months he says, "I went on the bum."

Stack is full of hobo stories, road stories of a time when he wasn't running for fun. He remembers regretfully when his best friend lay belly down on the top of a boxcar and the train passed through a tunnel. Could have been that Stack's friend just got curious at the precise instant that the train ripped through the opening of the tunnel—and he lifted up his head. Could have been that his friend pressed his face into the cold, rusted metal on top of the car but there wasn't enough room between his clinging body and the ceiling of the tunnel. Could have been a lot of things. Moments later, Stack found his friend's head.

He remembers sleeping in refrigerator cars and fitting himself into lumber cars like a two-by-four, in the foot-and-a-half space between the top of the lumber and the ceiling of the car. Cold times—up in North Dakota, 32 degrees below, climbing up the side of the car with fingers sticking to the rails like wet hands on a frozen ice tray.

Stack tells a story that he calls the "scariest and most unpleasant thing." He was riding on the Southern Pacific Railroad across the desert in Arizona sitting in a car in the dead center of the desert, in the dead heat of the day. A brakeman suddenly grabbed him and told him to get off the train. The train was rattling at top speed. Stack didn't know what to do. He was too scared to jump and didn't believe the man would force him off. Stack looked down at the ground. It sped past him like someone speeded up a film projector; only this wasn't a movie and he knew the ground was moving too fast to get a toe hold on, and he knew that if he jumped, the indifferent earth would speed up and smash him with the force of the train racing through the desert.

The brakeman threatened him. Stack didn't budge. The brakeman moved toward him. Stack sat still. They stared at each other the way animals stare before one decides to run, the other to kill. The brakeman kicked him off the train.

Stack wasn't hurt but he knew he was lucky. "There must be a better way to live," he thought. He tried the army but soon "got disgusted with it." With nowhere to go, and nothing to sustain him but his youth and health, Stack was taken by romance and decided it was time to go to sea. He had no credentials as a seaman. He had never been to sea before. But once he was onboard he figured he'd fake it enough to get by.

Throughout his youth, Stack developed a social conscience that became manifest while working in the shipping industry. He was involved in the labor movement. He became more radical when he thought his union, the MFOW (Marine Firemen, Oilers, Wipers, and Watertenders), was ineffective in bringing about any radical social change. He has worked hard for workingmen's rights most of his life. Former International Longshoremen's and Warehousemen's Union President Harry Bridges has called him "a great man who's never wavered in his principles over the years. He's fought for the things he's believed in and has made invaluable contributions to the working man."

Stack is dormant now. A pickup truck sideswiped him while he was riding his bicycle a few months back. He fell, broke four ribs, and suffered some cuts and scrapes. It really hurt. It hurt every time he took a breath. A few days before, with his ribs still smarting slightly, he ran 8 miles around a track. It felt good. A month's inactivity is difficult for someone as active as Stack.

Stack's exercising didn't begin at age fifty-eight. He always liked hiking, bicycling and swimming and played at all three whenever there was time. Before he started running, swimming was his favorite. In the 1950s when he was occasionally out of work, he swam some laps at the Fleishhacker pool in San Francisco. While swimming there, he met a lifeguard who told him about the Dolphin Swim Club. Stack joined and later met friends who ran to improve their swimming. He tried running. He tried it slowly; slowing his runs down with occasional walks. "It was tiring at times but never what you would call a struggle," he told his biographer Bob Bishop. "People I ran with kept telling me that running was fun; I had no idea what they were talking about. When they tried to get me to do another lap with them, no was the answer they always got from me."

Stack began to like it and running soon supplanted swimming as his primary sport. Although he has been forced off the road with his injury, he usually doesn't let anything prevent him from running. Twice before he was injured, once while running, another time when he rode his bicycle into an open manhole. Both mishaps detoured Stack some but he ran anyway with a neck brace and a cast on his broken wrist.

Beyond Stack's bedroom there is a roof that he frequently uses to sun his weary body. Sitting there, sunning with Stack, we asked him why he runs. "Running gives an ego a big boost. I don't make a principle of humility. There are some people who run for pleasure, to reduce tension, to stay healthy. But this marathoning is something different. They are for people who are looking for a challenge . . . I must accept a challenge . . . There is a great feeling of pleasure, in this acclaim, this glory, this recognition . . . What I do is bordering on the exhibitionist . . . One word will sum it up. Ego. Just plain ego."

"Ego," he says. I remember Stack's trophy room. I had seen a desk, a bookshelf crammed with books and on the outside wall, a large mirror. But mostly, there were trophies. Running trophies. Multicolored ribbons of recognition. Certificates of merit and service to the running community. Swimming trophies.

In Stack's bedroom there are shelves lined with running shoes. Two dozen pair. They all have different foreign names. They are all covered with plastic glue that Stack puts on where the shoe usually wears down. They were given to Stack by various shoe companies who hope that Stack's celebrity will sell their shoes.

On the bedroom wall there is a resolution from the Missouri House of Representatives. It states in part: "Be it resolved that the members of the Missouri House of Representatives, Eightieth General Assembly; First Regular Sessions; hereby extend a warm welcome to Mr. Walter Stack and commend him for his tremendous physical fitness efforts; and further extend their best wishes for continued great success in all future endeavours . . ."

I imagined him running across the San Francisco Bay Bridge, at five in the morning, with the sun just streaking past the metal cables on the bridge and the people in their limping cars squinting out their windshields—not sure of what they are seeing at first, because they are barely this side of their beds—and they are looking at the "old man" who's jogging across the bridge like it's high noon and everybody should be

Walter Stack running in San Francisco. (LORRAINE RORKE)

alive and awake; it's already five in the morning. Some of them wave. Some of them even smile and say hello because they know that this "old man" is as regular as the traffic jams, runs without fail week after week, with a cast or neck brace or hangover or anything.

Meanwhile, I pictured Stack thinking now about how his body feels, monitoring things (not too stiff today) . . . then about the friend who passed away (not an unusual event for a man Stack's age) . . . then his ribs that still hurt some . . . His foot is a little cramped. His shoulder stiff. The air is clear and he's taking large gulps of it, thinking about his labored breathing and the story of him in the magazine on the newsstand . . . then his dead friend again . . . then his running and feeling good, the cool rivulets of sweat, running across the Golden Gate Bridge at sunup with everyone half-asleep and the morning air soft all around him. At seventy-one, he feels awake and healthy and well—superior—as most runners do, as if they are part of some kind of physical elite that is thinner and calmer and healthier, and, even more righteous than the rest.

I wondered if ego drives him out of his warm bed at 2:30 A.M. to begin his daily workout. Most people would need more than ego, I thought. They would need a nuclear explosion. "You have to set a goal," Stack says. "With a goal you get motivation . . . When I tell people I'm going to run a 50-miler, I don't want anyone thinking, 'see that old man he tried to train for a 50-miler but he couldn't do it' . . . You've got to make up your mind. You've got to be determined . . . You've got to have strong motivation. It had to almost be an obsession."

Still, Stack looks away as he tells us he is not humble. Not knowing us, he's not sure how we're going to react to his defense of egotism. When we tell him he's one of the great-est athletes of his age in America, he's uncomfortable. When we tell him his legs are among the finest we've seen on any athlete, he shuffles his feet and grins, sheepishly.

He does all this, labels himself a turkey and expects us to believe he "doesn't make a principle of humility." Yet there's the trophy room. The talk of egotism and of training hard because other people might start thinking the old man can't do it. I tried to reconcile the two. I ended up figuring out that his humility is like the high school kid's who's just been told that he's not only the best-looking boy in the school but also the best athlete. He's embarrassed, genuinely so. He might even blush or fake an embarrassed grin. But he loves it just the same and he'll work hard to hear the compliments again.

Stack makes a principle of boosting other people's egos. As running commissioner of the Dolphin South End (DSE) Running Club, he is in a position of supporting collapsible egos. He has been called "the greatest feminist among us" by Joan Ullyot, author of *Women's Running*. Stack was one of the first men to fight for women's participation in running. In the DSE Stack insisted from the beginning that women and men should be awarded equal numbers of winners' ribbons even though a small minority of the runners were women. "I never knew how little self-esteem women had," Stack says. He speaks of women runners with affection. "I try to encour-age them. I come up from behind them and shout 'You're not going to let the old man beat you, are you.' It is all a matter of priorities," he scoffs.

Stack's friend Jay Longacre once told me one of his favorite Walter Stack stories. Stack stood on a picnic table giving instructions to runners gathered for a 5-mile run in San

Francisco. As always, he pointed out celebrities in the crowd, and created new ones by exaggerating accomplishments. But mainly, he was just fooling around, and raising hell and making people laugh.

The race was supposed to begin at eleven and it was already quarter after. Some of the runners were getting restless and told Stack to get things moving. Stack cut his speech short. He didn't want to upset anyone, even though he was just joking and having a good time.

He put his hands on the edge of the back of his pants and leaned forward about 20 degrees. "O.K. ladies and gentlemen," he said, "cover your eyes now, I'm going to take off my pants."

Now Stack is known for his antics. They're all good-natured, all part of his cheerful personality. But Walter Stack can surprise you. When Stack threatened to drop his running drawers you'd never know what was going to happen. Everyone kind of half-laughed and stared.

Stack took down his warmup pants and revealed his running shorts underneath. There was a group sigh. Then everyone sort of laughed slapping their bare knees. When everyone calmed down Stack ran past the crowd to the starting line and shouted what he always says at the beginning of a race. "Remember you hotshots. It's us turkeys in the back that make you look good."

The curious crowd followed. Stack then took off across the starting line, way out in front, and bellowed a harsh go . . . the race had officially begun.

Stack is now retired as a hod carrier. He remains active in union affairs. He still works on Fridays, teaching retarded adults how to swim. He gets out of bed at 5 A.M. now, to continue the same workout he's been accustomed to for fourteen years. He feels great. His weight is 160. Only 21 percent of his body is fat. His pulse rate is a phenomenal 40. Just last year he ran in the Western States 100-mile run: one of "the meanest, toughest, nastiest" footraces in the United States through the Sierra foothills.

Stack had decided to run the course because he thought, "Maybe those mountains will teach me a little humility." After 38 hours and 30 minutes from the cold start at dawn, Stack and his friend Jim Fauss crossed the finish line in a town named Auburn. Pat Smith, who came in an hour before, was the first woman to finish the course. Stack's abdominal muscles hurt for days. "Well you old fella," Stack said to himself. "You shouldn't be getting into these things with the younger fellas." Stack was then seventy years old.

That same year Stack ran nearly 5,000 miles with a 26.2 marathon per month marking his phenomenal effort.

Stack is very much aware that his body will begin to fail, that he is considered now, in numbers, an old man. He foresees cutting back on his mileage in a few years. "I'll run as long as I can," he says.

At the end of a recent marathon he checked himself to see if he was hurting more than usual. He wasn't. Yet he still is careful, never running hard. It's not healthy for an old man, he says. But he backs up. There was one time—He grins, that mischievous, wry, boyish grin of his, when a good story is coming. He was ending a marathon, he said, and this kid with long hair passed him and he said something like, what's the matter old man. Can't you make it!

Well Stack got mad and started to sprint. He didn't wave. He didn't smile and sip beer and "hot dog" it up like he usually does at the end of a marathon. No, the "turkey" caught a draft of air, swooped down on the back of the lean kid with the long blonde hair, running, driving his legs like a jackhammer until his lungs were whistling, until his gnarled legs hardened on the hot asphalt and he flew past the finish line, before the kid with the long hair.

We were leaving. Stack had to attend a union meeting. His wife came in, said hello and offered us some peaches. She is a pleasant woman who likes to make fun of her husband's achievements. When she heard we were writing about her husband, she said: "Well that's nice. I don't think he's a great marathoner though." Stack added again, "I'm just a turkey."

I wondered about it. I've know some real turkeys. I couldn't think of any of those birds who spend a lifetime working at something they believed in. None had ever forced themselves out of bed at 2:30 in the morning to work out before work. And not one, and this is for sure, ever had the fun-loving, invincible smile that tells you there is a lot of life in this chronologically old man. If *this* guy's a turkey, I thought, what does that make you and me?

R.M.

Jay Longacre

IN PURSUIT OF AN
ADVENTURE RUNNER

REMEMBER the Roadrunner cartoons that they used to show at movie theaters: Roadrunner if he catches you you're through? Roadrunner and his pursuer Wyle E. Coyote—sly, scheming—employing his wily ways to catch his speedy and elusive prey. Wyle E. always in pursuit—Roadrunner *Mmbeep—beep swoosh*—always just out of reach. Roadrunner fleeing through deserts and up mountains and rocketing from cliff to precipitous cliff. Coyote right behind him, racing over the cliffs, floating in midair, scrambling for safety—"Good heavens"—and smashing into the canyon floor with a *kaboom* and a puff of distant desert dust.

Well. It was that crazy cartoon I kept thinking about, running in the mountains of Santa Fe, New Mexico, chasing a real-life roadrunner, the pioneer adventure runner, Jay Long-acre.

I didn't want to catch him. I just wanted to keep up with him. My assignment was to talk with him, to learn about adventure running. Under the circumstances shouting my interview would have been more appropriate. I was after him Wyle E. Coyote style.

Jay Longacre runs in locations and for distances that are considered a feat to walk. He's run in the Himalayas in Nepal. He's run up Mt. Kilimanjaro in Africa. He's run up the Mauna Loa volcano in Hawaii—a place, as Longacre says, where there are "no trees, no grass, no one. Just you and the sun and the volcano."

Most of all, he's run in the United States. In the Pine Barrens of New Jersey. On the Monterey Peninsula and the Sierra Mountains of California. Up Mt. Washington in New Hampshire, along the Grand Canyon and on the seventy-five trails in and around his home in Colorado Springs, Colorado. He'll run anywhere "where there is an element of mystery or the unknown involved which represents some sort of challenge for a runner." There are all of these requirements in Santa Fe, New Mexico.

In 1926, a *New Mexican* editorial column reprinted a list of Santa Fe's special assets, as given in *Santa Fe: The Autobiography of a Southwestern Town*, by Oliver La Farge. They were Antiquity; old landmarks; a stirring history; a foreign flavor; a Spanish atmosphere; Pueblo Indians; a unique type of architecture; traditional and picturesque customs; a group of creative people, artists, writers, sculptors, musicians, architects; individuality, unconventionality and picturesqueness in dress; a remarkable array of native talent; a cosmopolitan population; a democratic social atmosphere founded on individuality and not money.

These are still there but a present editor might add a few more observations: a lot of money in the area; very expensive houses; houses of a reddish brown adobe that are of such a natural shape and color that they seem to rise up like mounds out of the ground; hippies; kids riding in shiny cars with the chassis barely off the street; fine restaurants; rounded green- and gold-covered mountains surrounding the city.

Longacre, his wife Barbara, my brother and myself—acquaintances last night but by now cohorts in adventure—drive through the green and gold and the shadow, up "Old Baldy," the oldest mountain in Santa Fe. There are a number of old baldies in the United States according to Longacre. The name is usually given to a worn, rounded mountain that is considered old in geologic time, in time immemorial. That is, old by our standards: approximately 70 million years.

Old Baldy is shining. With its center bulging up to 12,000 feet and some of its trails rocky and recently cut, it doesn't seem old to me. More middle-aged. But I am from the east where all mountains are considered old.

It is a sunny day and cloudless. The air is 80 degrees and dry, always dry, with everything snapping like pretzels under your feet. There are gold chamiso flowers and violet asters along the paved road that leads to the top of the mountain. They shimmer and flash. There are white aspens that lean but remain erect. They are still in the dry, windless air. With fall coming, the leaves are changing color, colors creating brilliant gold patterns like murals on the mountain wall.

Seven thousand feet. Longacre stops his AMC Pacer and we get out. Barbara will drive the car down the mountain and

Jay Longacre. (LARRY EVANS)

wait for us. There is talk of our "upcoming ordeal." We stretch. The air is thin here. We start out and my lungs immediately begin to burn: a burning reminiscent of the feeling in my throat after swimming a long distance or breathing in cold, dry air. I fill up my lungs twice; I hope that two will be the equivalent to one at sea level. No relief. They still burn.

Longacre, meanwhile, is spreading his arms and loosening his legs. He "belly breathes," forcing out carbon dioxide, while pushing the stomach muscles down simultaneously to prevent abdominal cramps. We blow out hard in unison. We reach a steep downhill, running and talking to Longacre up until this point but as we run over the top, it is *Mmbeep—beep* Jay Longacre, his arms dropped extremely low and loose at his sides, his head upright, chest out, leaning forward, literally falling down the hill.

On a flat surface, say a street or a field, some runners look like they're skimming and gliding; their bodies, in the air half the time, are almost vertical. Not Longacre. He runs tilted forward, determined looking, about 15 degrees from an upright position. His arms and legs are relaxed and rhythmic but they seem to reach and dig in the manner of a person running up a steep incline. It is as if Longacre has run so many miles uphill that he is, in style at least, always running uphill.

The downhill is different. He runs "the downhills in doubletime. The trick is to work with gravity," Longacre shouts from a distance. "Don't fight the hill! Don't fight yourself! Get your body perpendicular to the hill and relax; always relax; most people apply their brakes on the hill; let yourself go; let gravity do the work; don't ever walk down a hill; walk up the hill and then run down the hill."

So. Here we are, my lungs are still burning, some alien fire raging without oxygen, following Longacre's lead, falling down the mountain like a rock.

Longacre is out in front, plummeting to a gradual slow-down on a flat ridge as far as I can see. We are falling and floundering, out of control, like running on a treadmill you can't get off. "Good heavens." Fortunately, at the bottom, catastrophe is averted. There is no Coyote *kaboom*.

Both failure and success have taught Longacre many of his adventure running techniques. He once was caught with a twisted ankle and thin cotton clothing, 15 miles up Rampage Road in the Garden of the Gods park in Colorado. It was getting dark and cold. The temperature dropped from 65 to 30 degrees in an hour. His ankle was swelling. He couldn't run. His sweat cooled. He couldn't stay warm. He walked down the mountain, shivering, looking for his wife whom he was supposed to meet at the bottom. She picked him up, finally, took him home and helped him into a bathtub. He was in the bathtub for an hour and a half before he could say a coherent word.

In the winter he always wears wool now: wool sweaters, long wool underwear and wool socks on his hands. "They're cheaper than wool mittens," he says. He then covers the wool insulation with a Gor-tex rain suit. In the mountains, when the sun is shining at high altitudes, he wears a pair of sunglasses that he bought after a case of snow blindness: a burning of the eyes caused by the reflection of the sun off the snow in high altitudes. In the desert he wears a beaked hat that shades his face and a thin turtleneck to keep the sun off his neck.

In the spring of 1978, Longacre attempted to run 150 miles from Katmandu in Nepal to Mt. Everest base camp. It was an outlandish idea. Perilous. Unthinkable. To Longacre "fun" and certainly "a challenge." He had heard of hikers walking the route. No one he knew "had actually run it" before.

Longacre usually has difficulty getting information for his adventure runs. He searches for relevant books, articles and government pamphlets; he wants to get a sense of the people, the culture and their language. He checks air force reconnaisance maps and consults with people who are familiar with the chosen terrain; he wants to know the shape of the land, the altitude and the actual distance of the run. Vital information is scarce. His last resort is to rely on tips from backpackers whose advice is not always accurate.

For this run he was fortunate. He met a member of the American Centennial Everest Expedition—Jerry Roach—who gave him information on the physical geography of the area. He read a dozen books on Nepal and conferred with numerous doctors on their views on high-altitude exertion. His plans were to leave in April, before the monsoon season but not before the Boston Marathon.

He ran the Boston Marathon in a PR, (personal record), of 2:55 and left directly for Katmandu. There, in a city of 300,000 people and an altitude of 4,200 feet, Longacre was slowed by heavy snow. He relaxed, spending the next few days enjoying the Nepalese people and the white crystalline mountains that surrounded him.

"The Nepalese are the kindest people I've ever met," says Longacre. "They are more relaxed than people in the United States. Their religion and customs make them a calm people . . . In the mountains they know how to help you if you are hurt. Villagers get together, feed you and gather people to carry you out."

Longacre has never needed them for anything more than

food and shelter. He knows, in the case of an accident, however, that they will always be there to help. His extensive preparation and his persistent mental and physical conditioning, he says, protects him from grave injury. Indeed, from death.

For the Himalayan run he trained every day, 150 miles a week, often running up steep hills and through deep snow at altitudes of 9,600 and 12,000 feet. His mental preparation was a daily process, too. "I've concluded," Longacre says, "that running is 2 percent diet, 8 percent physical and 90 percent psychological (rational, emotional, spiritual). Three hundred days out of the year my attitude is positive," he says. "Negative thoughts are a waste of time. You have to train your mind, relax your mind. You can't abuse yourself. You have to get yourself tough and utilize your ability to take stress when you have to. I can go without sleep for a night and not feel bad the next day. But that is because for months previous to that sleepless night I was getting the right amount of rest."

A night came with a full moon—what Longacre had been waiting for. It was Saturday, April 22, 1978. The white spires of the Himalayas loomed ahead of him. He set out on a metallic path with the moonbeams following him. He wore stars-and-stripes running shorts, a wool sweater, flat shoes, nylon rainsuit, with a cup, a pint of water and $8 in rupees. He carried a flashlight, an air force map and a note written in Nepalese: "Please help this man. He is running as quickly as he can to Kala Pattar, near Everest. Do not disturb him. If you want to talk with him, please wait until he comes back."

Twelve miles into the mountains, in the moonlight darkness, he arrived at a village that he assumed incorrectly was Dologot. He wanted to find some tea but the only place that was open would not serve him. He asked villagers what town he was in. "Dologot?" he asked. "No Bonope," they said. He had taken the wrong shortcut. He was only halfway to Dologot.

With "incredible blisters" and a thirst that foced him to drink any water he could find, risking diarrhea, he continued on through the night searching for the correct route to Dologot.

He described his run in an article in *Runners World* magazine.

"A woman comes out of one of the houses and sees me in my American flag shorts, a red cap and a singlet with Colorado on it and is scared to death. Finally, her husband comes out and I ask him where the heck the trail is. Most of the people over there only know their village, the one before it and the one after it—nothing else—but he sent me off the mountain looking for the trail. I tried several routes but continually kept getting lost. There was nothing I could do so I just sat down by the side of the river and threw stones until sunrise."

In the morning, he found porters who lead him to the right trail. He ran on then, from 2,000 to 7,500 feet, through a "big swatch" with moist red clay and loose rocks "the size of watermelons." Then, the path became part of a clear creek bed with water from a higher source rushing down at him—a sucking implosion of water. He leaped from rock to slippery rock trying to avoid the torrent beneath him.

He soon learned what running in Nepal was really like: "You go up a mountain, over the top, down the other side, cross the river, up another mountain, down it, cross another river and you do this all day."

The third day then. The sun set fire to the peaks above him, the air was thin and still. He set out taking deep "drags" of it and exhaling slowly. His smoky senses immediately began to clear. He was, in the lingo of the drug culture, high.

"You see the white and the colors. I saw the rhododendrons and the snow. Wow, the Himalayas—that snow!

"The rhododendron trees were above 10,000 feet. Red and pink and white. They are gorgeous. And butterflies and birds. And pheasants of unusual size and color."

Longacre was not on drugs. It was a different high than any drug experience. The shape and the flash were not artificial. The snow did not look dazzling because of a drugged brain. And the excited quickening heart was not caused by an alien chemical. Longacre says it's oxygen. Oxygen taken in large doses, in gusts, like a cool wind following a storm that leaves everything bright and shimmering.

"I saw a vulture about 20,000 feet. He must have had an 8-foot wing span. He went over the mountain like a shot, he never seemed to flap his wings."

It began to rain. The light show was temporarily turned off. The road was muddy. He had to find shelter for a while but soon he was out on a path for another 20 miles that day.

The following days were dreary. Tired and unravelled, he ran on through three rainstorms, two snowstorms and high altitudes that affected his moods. He weakened at times; his head whirling. Resolve kept him going.

One night, up in the thickly clouded mountains, he ran with a horrendous case of diarrhea and with snow coming at him so hard he couldn't see. He spent the night in a tea house, lying on a hard wooden board shivering. "I kept telling myself to get up and stretch and exercise but I was so cold I couldn't move. I knew that's the kind of thing—not moving—that kills people but all I could do was shiver. It was horrible."

Meanwhile, his wife Barbara waited in a monastery a few days' walk from Namche Bazaar. She was worried. She was supposed to meet her husband in Namche Bazaar but he never arrived.

"I do the worrying," she once told me. "My husband is the most positive person I know. He never looks at the bad things in life."

Distracted, tense, she waited in the monastery. Her Sherpa guide, Gyalzen, told her he had a dream that Jay was fine, that he was certain that he would be in Namche Bazaar that night. Gyalzen waited for Longacre in town. Longacre never came.

The following day she "couldn't bear the tension anymore." She decided to look for him in Namche Bazaar.

She met hikers on the way down and asked where they were from.

"Germany and Israel and England," they told her. "Where are you from," they asked. "America," she answered. "You must be Mrs. Longacre," they said. "We spent last night listening to your husband's fantastic tale of his adventure in Kala Pattar."

"I was ecstatic," Mrs. Longacre said. "He's alive, he's well and he made it to Kala Pattar." "How is he," she asked. "Fine. A cold and sore feet are all."

Longacre realized Gyalzen's dream, passing through the town of Namche Bazaar the night before. Jay if you meet Barbara here, he thought to himself, and spend the night with a warm bed and warm food, the way you feel, you're not going to get up in the morning. Jay you'd better go for it now.

Not far from the end, after running for almost four days,

past sixty-four villages, across twenty-four rivers, he was tired of thin air and soggy ground, of snow and rain and feeling sick—of running. He was near exhaustion. His head was reeling. "I just wanted to lay down and die. I remember leaning against this rock, looking at Mt. Everest and being so dog tired that I didn't even know I could stay awake. I took my pulse and it was 60. Sixty! Here I was at 18,200 feet, thinking I'm near death and my . . . pulse is at 60. All of a sudden I started feeling elated, I felt great!"

Twenty-four hours later, after 19 miles running to the top of Kala Pattar and back down to Namche Bazaar, he was truly exhausted. His feet were "in terrible shape." His wife's Sherpa guide, Gyalzen, the holder of the record for the opposite route, helped him to a room in the International Footrest Motel. His body stiffened as Gyalzen helped him peel off his clothes and bathe out of a dishpan.

He found accommodations, finally, at the hotel. He talked several hours with guests and ate and sipped tea. He ate yak steak, whole-wheat spaghetti with yak meal sauce and rice pudding. He ate ravenously, attempting to regain some of the 20 pounds he lost on the journey.

The next morning he was amazed at how good he felt. He "would have run back to Katmandu," if his feet were in better shape.

The next year he ran again. This time he took six experienced American marathon runners along with him. After the first day, they were sore, irritable and sick with diarrhea. The following morning they refused to go on. Longacre says they rejected the antibiotics that would have prevented the water from poisoning their systems. Some were sick for six weeks afterwards.

Born in Wilmington, Delaware, Longacre never ran as a boy. "Physical education teachers always associated exercise with suffering and punishment," Longacre says. "It wasn't supposed to be fun."

At thirty-one, on April Fools Day 1967, Longacre ran out to the road for some suffering and punishment. He was feeling fat and lazy. "I knew I was getting bad when I started asking my children to turn the channel on the television for me." At 5'7" he weighed 180 pounds. His waist was 38 inches in circumference. He whizzed and trudged around the block once. Not much fun. He whizzed and trudged the next day. Still no fun. But he says he "didn't give up and now with over ten years and 42,000 miles passed, running is fun." So much so that Longacre's life has radically changed because of it. His weight is now 146. His resting pulse rate is 38. A lawyer–fundraiser, Longacre now works independently in real estate and in freelance fundraising work for nonprofit organizations. He put his four children through school, divorced, remarried and moved to Colorado Springs where he could train in high altitudes. He is now planning to move to Sante Fe, New Mexico where he can run in the mountains there and enjoy his passion for art.

Longacre is telling me his story in Sante Fe; telling it as he bounds up a steep, spiraling path, with the sureness of a Himalayan blue sheep. We help each other through a barbed wire fence. Part of the adventure.

By now I am suffocating from the altitude. My head throbs and heaves in sync with my steps. I force a few resuscitative breaths. My lungs wheeze. No use. Someone has cut my respirator. I am one huge, thumping heart.

We head over the top of Old Baldy, my brother and I,

Jay Longacre leading author Morrissey (last) and another runner across a mountain in Colorado.

staccato stepping. The downhill provides some relief. Long-acre is "loping," touching down shortly and bouncing back up for a floating breath, like a moonwalker. He executes this improvised run-hop with his arms spread out and his weight dropping on one foot in a springing action. The idea is to ensure your footing among the rocks and to gain as much distance through leaping and floating.

I can't run. Too many obstacles. I'm hot but I don't seem to sweat; the sweat evaporates as soon as it surfaces leaving a shoreline of salt on my clothes. I walk through dry gullies, snapping dead branches, and weave through sharp-hooked bushes. I watch, as Longacre, now the halfback, blasts through the line of trees, stiff arming branches, dodging aspens. Bush-wacking. I'm feeling the altitude. The slightest turn of my ankle or prick from a defensive bush ignites a strange fury in me. My brother's flammatory mood is more vocal. You crazy . . . he shouts at Longacre. I laugh at his brashness. I'm feeling small and tentative, thinking of a tiny, frantic spider I saw crossing Interstate 10 enroute from Texas to Sante Fe. It moved erratically. Scurrying. Stopping. Scurrying. Spiders can only see a few inches in front of them. So—myopic, whimsical—it groped across the highway oblivious to the steel belted blow that was about to smash it into the concrete.

Altitude affects people in various ways. It has ruined mountain expeditions and was one of the causes for the group failure of Longacre's second Himalayan run. "Altitude impairs your judgment," Longacre says. You get a depressed feeling, thinking what am I doing here. But, I know what it is. I understand it and when it happens I sort of laugh at myself and keep on running.

I laughed at my low spirits—still thinking of the spider —and resumed running.

We finished the race after a long, long uphill. Looking up, I saw an oil-black slab that rose to a blue sky so clear it seemed to have no depth: some sort of bruising pathway to running heaven.

Longacre thinks about his running when he runs. When the pain gets bad, real bad, he thinks about it some more, either changing his form to stop the pain or mentally driving the pain out: associative running.

Many runners do the opposite. They disassociate, hoping that while they're not paying attention the pain will go away and their bodies will function normally again. I am a disassociator. I am fantasizing now to the point of seeing painkilling mirages. Most of them are cool, watery images but some are of the censorable variety. I copied Longacre, crisscrossing the hill to make the ascent seem easier. I stared at my rickety legs and feet. I couldn't bear to look up.

Every drained cell in my body says stop—20 miles is enough—what do you think you are, a camel or something, but it hurts too much to stop. I fear collapse, dry ice will form on my lungs, my muscles will cramp up and my vital organs will arrest and die. So—for survival reasons, I have to keep going, have to keep the air flowing, flowing through my lungs like water through the gills of a shark.

In town. In an oasis of a pizzeria, Longacre stands with a slightly sadistic grin on his face. Like most runners, he has a different concept of pain than most people do. "Pain is relative," Longacre says. In other words, you don't concern yourself with it, you just keep running. Longacre drinks four large Cokes and a large iced tea. I drink water. My parched throat widens and erodes as I drink. Longacre gulps and talks and laughs and gulps some more as I sit suffering and sipping.

Longacre drinks tea—a whole tide of it in one sitting. After around a half a dozen cups, his thirst will recede. I'd like to wean myself from this tea, he says. Tea is about his only bad habit, he says. He eats a high complex carbohydrate diet: a lot of pasta, chicken and fish. Once, after a marathon, he drank twelve Cokes. "I got so gorged I had to lay down and rest a while."

8 A.M.: the second day in Sante Fe. We're out for a short 5-mile run and I am chased by bloodhounds. Not exactly getting lost in the Himalayas but adventure enough to start. They are friendly bloodhounds, fortunately. Big, black, lanky beasts with hanging ears and red, wet tongues. They embrace me in the attitude of an old friend, wrapping their paws around my shoulders and slobbering kisses all over my face. I stiffen, looking at them bewildered and frightened, not knowing whether to dance for our reunion or decline in ignorance of any past friendship. At last, they leave me alone. They must realize they are on the wrong scent. It's him you're after, I say, pointing to Longacre. A case of mistaken identity.

One hundred yards down the road behind me, a German shepherd, his head low, lopes from scent to scent, sniffing the bottoms of trees. When he sees me up ahead he stiffens. He waits a second, his head high. Then he takes off to join the greeting party.

When I see him lunge towards me, adrenaline squirts through my arteries. I feel it shoot up the back of my neck and spread out across my shoulders. I feel it needling my fingertips. I dash out of there without saying goodbye to my friends.

There is a human response to stressful situations that has

been part of our body chemistry for, perhaps, millions of years. It is called the flight or fight response. A book, *The Relaxation Response*, describes this process. "When we are faced with situations that require adjustment of our behavior, an involuntary response increases our blood flow to the muscles, and metabolism, preparing us for conflict or escape . . . This innate flight or fight reaction is well recognized in animals. A frightened cat standing with arched back and hair on end, ready to run or fight; an enraged dog with dilated pupils snarling at his adversary; an African gazelle running from a predator; all are responding by activation of the flight or fight response."

Well, when that German shepherd came after me and I realized, looking back, that he wasn't trying to catch me just to say hello and smooch a little bit, and when I heard that harsh *roo roo* roar behind me, I blasted out of there like my blood was made of pure alcohol and liquid oxygen, catching up in an instant to Longacre who couldn't figure out what the heck had gotten into me. Must of loosened up, he probably thought. I played along with him, as if I do the 100-yard dash in 10 seconds all the time.

Longacre's running has led him to flee from more than a mere domestic dog. In Africa, on Mt. Meru in Tanzania, he came down a large scree slide that led into a lush meadow. There were rocks, branches and deep jeep tracks. He had to keep his head down and watch his footing. He glanced up to see where he was going, and up ahead about 100 yards, standing on the edge of the thick woods, was a big, brown bull elephant. Longacre stopped. He didn't dare move. Handling a bull elephant takes a little bit more care and finesse than handling your basic neighborhood bow-wow. The elephant swung his huge trunk around. Longacre looked around for a convenient tree to scuttle up. It would have been time to play Tarzan if the elephant had charged. But the elephant didn't move. He either didn't see Longacre or wasn't bothered by Longacre's rapid intrusion. He shifted a ton of weight on one foot then lumbered off into the woods, out of sight.

Again, in the same meadow, running in high grass, a leopard leaped out in front of him. "I didn't hear a twig snap. He went by in a flash and I didn't hear him. I was nervous getting through that grass. My palms were sweating. There were animals all over the place." In that one day he saw about fifteen hundred animals.

His palms were sweating! There are runners who become rabid at the sight of a miniature poodle after them and here's Longacre, confronting a bull elephant and a leaping leopard and the only flight or fight response characteristics he's affected by are a little nervousness, a little sweaty palms.

Longacre realizes that his perilous adventure running is not for everyone. His misadventures would scare away anyone. But you don't have to travel to Nepal and endanger your life to enjoy adventure running. There is adventure, Longacre says, right outside your door.

"You can run in your friends' backyard. They can run in yours. For both it is an adventure. You have to use your imagination. Your definition of adventure running will change as you run . . . Vary the speed. Vary the direction. Vary the circumstances. Today I want to run where I saw the deer in the woods. Today I want to run into the village to see some friends. Running in a snowstorm can be an adventure. The possibilities increase as you run. Running isn't boring. You are boring. Take a look at what it is in front of you. Think about what you see."

Longacre is a calm and spirited man, characteristics that

cannot be separated from his running. He talks with a western drag, the words running into each other occasionally and when he's run and he's relaxed—more relaxed—he drags the words out so his speech begins to singsong a bit and the sentences sometimes end with a soft, velvety voice that people often use before they go to sleep.

He isn't falling asleep though. He thinks and talks at his own pace. When the topic of art comes up, he's interested by the different levels of interpretation. When the topic of running is raised, he's getting excited, his voice rises. "The best contribution that an individual can make to society is to stay healthy . . . Running is fun. But I also run for endurance and strength and health. The idea is to be able to run for your whole life. Adventure running is something you can do for your whole life. I hope to be healthy when I'm eighty. People ask me if I'm afraid if all this running is going to kill me. Well, I know one thing, if it does kill me and I doubt very much that it will, I'm going to enjoy the time I'm alive."

When he talks of running's potential, of people's potential for self-fulfillment, he really gets rolling. "Train your mind to think positively," he says. "You might think that talk of positive thinking is corny; that all the books that are out on positive thinking are corny too. But live that way and it will work for you.

"Don't abuse yourself. Be good to yourself. Treat yourself by not drinking and smoking and eating bad foods. Don't do everything because everyone else wants you to do it. Be true to yourself. Stay engaged. Engaged in what is around you. Develop interests. Things that you develop yourself are important because no one can take them away from you. You have your health and your happiness. You know how to live. You will only see and experience a speck of the world in your lifetime. By God go after that speck."

Heavy stuff. Well, when he talks about adventure running, he exhorts us to look at how beautiful America is and to discover how much more of it could be seen through adventure running. Nothing too preachy, too righteous. He seems just to want people to enjoy what he enjoys, to look at what is in front of them. Adventure running is Longacre's way of seeing more.

Longacre is not short on oxygen nor is he "O'D'ing" on it. It is enthusiasm. Enthusiasm that is rare in a man forty-five years old. If he seems to jump off the mountain in his excitement over adventure running, what else can you expect from a proud father? I've heard worse from that group. But his positive attitude is not shallow and emptyheaded. Optimism is often considered that. Pessimism is somehow considered more sensitive, more intelligent. Many runners feel an occasional intoxication with life, as I suspect all athletes do, but popular reproach prevents them from saying anything that's too happy, too positive, making their exultant tongues stiffen.

Longacre's words are fluid and emotional. With a record that is evidence of the effectiveness of his attitude, you don't question the legitimacy of his argument, with the emotional words and the exuberant wake that follows even a skeptic like myself gets the feeling that what he says is genuine; that he lives by what he suggests for others and that if you listen, you'll hear of a route to greatness.

Longacre coaches young friends who would like to run in future marathons or even in high-altitude adventure running. He says to build a base of strength first. Run cross-country. Run long and slow. Run relaxed. Don't worry about speed . . . Run because you want to run not because someone else wants you to . . .

Longacre will probably take some young runners with him when he runs up the Mauna Loa volcano in Hawaii again this December. Last year, a park worker at the top of Mauna Loa saw him and said, "My lord some fellow just ran through here on a dead run." Longacre had erupted.

The mountain was immensely silent. The ground so barren it could have been Mars. Longacre passed rippling formations of lava and ran over "gravel substances the size of lemons. . ." The surface was difficult to run on. It was deceptive in its silence. "It [the mountain] was alive. I could feel it —could not see it—but nevertheless this mountain was moving. Its heart was on fire."

He finished running up and down the massive mountain in 7:20. He started at 6:45 A.M. and make it back just 5 minutes late for a luncheon with his wife at 2 P.M. The climb usually takes three days for competent hikers.

Longacre has plans for future adventure runs in Africa, in Burma, in Europe, all over the United States and with permission from the people in the Republic of China, in Tibet.

He wants to publicize adventure running, get it moving. He is convinced that adventure running is the "path" that the "running movement" will take. It will move alone, he says. But he wants to get behind it and encourage it some. He thinks that once people become tired of circling tracks and running themselves mad in 10 K races, they will look for something else; they will look towards adventure running, to the outdoors, where the spectators are indifferent but the variety of experience is infinite.

If he is right and adventure running becomes as popular

in America as road racing, the name Jay Longacre may become as familiar as Bill Rodgers or Frank Shorter, names revered in running circles and remembered as great in the history of the sport.

We are leaving Santa Fe, walking to our car with the heel-toe waddle of race walkers. Our thighs hurt too much to bend. (After a marathon, some runners have problems walking down stairs.)

We reach our car finally and the door won't open. In the delirium following our adventure run, we had locked our keys in the car. They are in view, shining on the dashboard. The windows are rolled tight. The lock is secure in the armrest. The car is owner-proof.

Longacre seems to like the challenge. He thinks of alternatives, of possibilities. "Call the locksmith," he says. "It's Sunday," I say. "Try his home," he says. "No answer," I report back. "Get a knife then," he says.

I run up, uh, hobble up to get a knife and slit the top of the door. We slip the hanger through the hole; it dangles near the lock. Longacre maneuvers the loop around the lock. Slips off. He maneuvers it again. It slips off again. Each time the loop is secure around the lock, we hold our breath and pull up. No luck.

We are despairing now. Longacre's got more ideas. We try the same method one more time, fastening the loop completely around the lock. Slowly now. Easy. We stopped to make sure it was done right. Someone's arm hits the hanger. "I always keep going," Longacre said once. "I never stop." The lock lifts and we open the door.

R.M.

Grete Waitz

THE SCANDINAVIAN WONDER

OFFICIALS in yellow jackets scurry at the finish line of the Moon Day Marathon in Long Island, New York. The sandy-haired leader is now in the distance, now drawing near. The crowd is overwhelming, ecstatic and, well . . . whacko. They lean over one another, arms flailing, shouting themselves mute. Some are dripping tears, laughing. It's a woman in the lead. She is on her way to becoming the first woman in marathon history to beat everyone—everyone including the four thousand men behind her who will never be the same again. Grete Waitz—the ruling "queen of distance running," crossed the finish line, with race workers rushing towards her, engulfing her. A woman winning the marathon? Pheidippides, that original marathon person, must be cramping up in his grave! Or, perhaps, he is clapping.

The race is an imaginary one. But only in the arrangement of realities. The fact is that Grete Waitz broke the women's world record in the 1979 New York City Marathon with a time of 2:27:33. That is approximately 5:38 per mile for 26.2 miles: 5:38, mile after draining mile, to the very welcome finish. It is a time that would have won the Olympic Marathon any year before 1952 and broke the world record in 1939. It was a time, more importantly, that would have won many of the three hundred and some marathons run this year in the United States.

The New York race was run on a course that is considered by some to be a terrible site for the felling of records. There are uneven streets. Potholed streets. Streets with man-

Grete Waitz.
(STEVE RONAGHAN)

hole covers and steel gratings. The footing at high speeds is erratic, unstable. Runners, preoccupied with their foot placement, may lose their timing and consequently their speed.

It was run, too, in unremitting heat. First in the morning, a steamy humidity. Then in the afternoon, a striking sun. The media were there, as always, enlarging the event. A huge beneficent crowd urged her to beat the men. And Grete Waitz placed in this unfamiliar sauna, placed in the position of Rocky taking on the established champ, still ran the distance faster than any woman before her. It was an indisputable declaration of all women's potential and one woman's talent and determination.

She looked in control as she ran through the yellow ribbon at the finish line. Her chest heaved as she caught her breath but smiled as race officials congratulated her. She looked less fatigued than most of the male finishers—including the winner for the fourth consecutive year, Bill Rodgers.

Inside the press room she sat with her hands clasped on her bare knees. Her posture was erect, dignified. She asked if it was all right to sit on the good furniture with her wet running shorts. She sat very still. Reporters from every medium jostled for position, leaning towards her. Their frantic movements exaggerated her poise. Thick black electrical cables circled her feet. Bright television lights beamed on and off her. The queen was holding court.

She listened smiling, her head cocked, listened with the concentrated look of a person who is not only hearing words but translating them. The questions were endless. Her control never quivered. She was still answering questions in her dim, polite voice as the last of the fifteen thousand runners crossed the finish line, five hours after the start of the race.

She does get tired. Tired of hearing the same questions, of talking about herself. A few hours after a marathon is one thing but the same inquiries never stop. She told *The Runner* magazine, "It is very strenuous spending the whole day speaking to people, always answering the same questions. . . It's not so easy always having people looking at you, talking to you."

She is a private person. She doesn't care to be a celebrity nor does she understand the American media's desire to celebrate her. But her want for privacy is overcome by her wish to please. "And you have to keep smiling at all the people; and if you don't do it, they say she is a bad girl."

She is a schoolteacher in Norway; she does what she thinks is right and fair. But as the interviewer immediately learns, she is not exactly enjoying these sessions.

I spoke with her a few weeks after the 1979 New York City Marathon. It was a time, I think, when Waitz was beginning to feel she was being held hostage by American journalists. She was stiff, guarded. It is times like these that the interviewer really feels he or she is intruding, prying into secret inviolate places. You ask questions tentatively, treading watchfully like a trespasser.

She talked in short, curt sentences. Her English was fluent, but she seemed uncomfortable with it. Her voice was high and sometimes breathless, like someone who has just come in from the cold. There were no extra words in her answers.

"Did you like California?" I asked.

"Yes," she said.

"What did you like about it?"

"It was warm," she said.

Nothing more. Nothing less. What you ask is what you get.

She is much prettier than most photographs of her suggest. They are usually tense, hard views of her straining at the end of a track race—or worse, a marathon. No one looks good at the end of a marathon. Her muscles are normally thin and unexaggerated. She is 5'7" 119 pounds. Her body is spare, legs long, hips narrow, her bone-squared shoulders form the base of her triangular torso. She wears no makeup. She has a soft, unmistakable Scandinavian face, and when her sandy hair is in pigtails and she lapses into a smile, a constrained smile, her reserved womanly look dissolves into the bright innocence of a young girl.

There is a correctness, a propriety about her that has been referred to as "stately." Fred Lebow, president of the New York Road Runners Club, probably knows Grete Waitz better than anyone in America, because of his contacts with her during the last New York City marathons. I asked him if she was always so shy and restrained. "She is reserved and carries herself in a regal manner," he said. "She is very well-liked in Europe. In a recent popularity poll in Norway she was voted the number one personality in the country. She is socially charming, but not one for small talk. If she were the queen of Norway she wouldn't act any differently. If you were to program a person in figure, looks and personality for the queen of the roads, it would be her."

Indeed, Waitz has proven to be a runner's paragon. She holds the world record in the 10- and 15-kilometer runs. She holds Norwegian records in 1,500 and 3,000 meters. She has run two marathons faster than any woman ever—4 minutes faster. She has won the world cross-country championships three years in a row and is the favorite to win and revise her own world record in the next New York City Marathon. She says she runs for fun.

For fun! The explanation, however true—and most top

competitors in the marathon say the same thing—shouldn't give the impression that Grete Waitz does not work hard. She has been training and competing for over thirteen years. Since 1975 she has run two workouts a day. Her running implies a lifestyle. There is time for running. Time for housework. Time for schoolteaching. All time is alloted, segmented. Nothing too rigid. Just a uniformity, a familiar daily design that allows for the smooth succession of responsibilities met, of goals achieved. Each season brings a new schedule.

In winter, (which starts in November), she leaves her husband in bed around 6 A.M. and takes off for the first run of the day. The roads are dark and vacant. The slanted winter light appears at 8:30 A.M. and will be gone by 4 P.M. Bare trees sway and clack in the cold. Waitz, dressed in two track suits, a wool cap and gloves, glides along the hardened snow, her rubber soles squeaking. Her breath clouds up. The cold stings her lungs. After 15 frozen kilometers, she is finished.

In the afternoon she runs long distance. Not long *slow* distance—what is called LSO. She "believes in quality not quantity. Too much long slow distance makes long slow runners," she says. She will average 120 to 140 kilometers per week.

In the spring, summer and fall there are variations on this steady routine. In the spring, when the snow recedes and the mud dries to a depth below her ankles, she runs in the woods. The distance is slightly shorter than in winter, but speed workouts are of a finer quality and more frequent. The summer is track season and speed is very important. At the end of the summer, her pace will slow. Long-distance runs, on and off the road, will prepare her for the road racing of the fall season.

In 1978, ten days before the October race, never having run more than 10 miles in competition and 13 miles in training, she decided to run the New York City Marathon. No one knew her then. A few officials and some of the top runners had heard of her success in European track but no one thought she had the training to run well in the marathon. No one but her husband Jack, who convinced her to come to New York to run and was equally convinced of her ability to win.

At the starting line, Waitz was confused, frantic—a lost traveler in a skittish crowd. She wrote in *New York Running News*, "But when we arrived at Staten Island, I felt very lonely. I didn't know what to do and I didn't know anybody. And when the gun went off I thought, 'Now you have three hours of hard work before you can rest.' "

At 18 miles she was second. Across the Queensboro Bridge, she approached the leader, Martha Cooksey. She felt good, running hard, enjoying the sights, her body loose and alive . . . But wait a second. This isn't the way Grete Waitz would tell this story. Her telling would be much more orderly, much more precise. She would start from the beginning.

Grete Anderson Waitz (pronounced whites) was born on October 1, 1953, in Oslo, Norway. Her father was a manufacturing pharmacist. Her mother worked in a grocery shop. Her parents didn't have much of an influence on her taking up athletics. But Oslo, a town of ski trails, ski jumps and very athletic inhabitants, surely affected the young girl.

Yet why did a great woman runner come from what we would call a ski town? Both of Grete's older brothers ski cross-country. Her husband Jack Waitz, who in addition to cross-country skiing often runs 50 or 60 miles a week himself, says Grete "might have a bigger talent for cross-country skiing." Part of the answer is Norwegian Sports Clubs. The clubs have a powerful influence in Norway. The Norwegian Confederation of Sports, a government-supported organization, encourages mass participation in all sports. Waitz joined the club early. Her friends did, too. Her fun, interest and achievement have since then always been in athletics.

The "tomboy" characterization doesn't apply here. Waitz's abilities developed unself-consciously. She tried all sports. Handball. Football. Waitz considers the idea "old-fashioned," that through athletics women become muscular and lose their femininity. The idea grew out-dated earlier in Norway than it did in the United States. Only recently have women in this country become comfortable with sweat and the hardened thigh.

In this supermarket of sports she chose running because she says, "My girlfriends were in the track and field club." She wasn't a star then: "Not pretty bad. Not pretty good," as she puts it. She high jumped, long jumped. "It was fun," she says. She was twelve years old.

Her talent evolved, and as a high follows a good run, her interest did also. "When I was fifteen or sixteen I won some races and that motivated me to train more. I did and my results improved. It was like a little snowball which grew bigger and bigger." And faster and faster.

Before she turned eighteen running remained "sport, fun, a game. We ran, played together. I was not serious." At eighteen she began to train hard. At twenty she started two workouts a day. She found she had more success as the distances increased.

In the 1976 Olympics the people of Norway expected much from the young track runner. In 1974, at the European Championships, she won a bronze medal in the 1,500 meters. The world considered her one of the best. The Norwegians considered her number one—a sure win for the gold medal in the Olympics.

Her subsequent defeat in the Olympic 1,500-meter hurt very much. She was fairly satisfied herself. She had rushed to a personal and national record of 4:04.8. But to the people in Norway, her rush should have brought home gold to her country.

"Just after the 1976 Olympics I was very disappointed. I did my best in the semifinal run, 4:04.8, a new Norwegian record, but I didn't qualify for the final which was my goal before the games. When I came home a lot of people told me that they were disappointed at what I did in the Olympics and that hurt me . . ."

The public criticism stopped her competitive running. Her serious training stopped. She ran for fun.

Oslo is a city of forests. Our conceptions of city and forest, of cement and trees, make that seem impossible, like predator and prey living peaceably. But Oslo is one of the least urbanized cities in the world. Nature although slightly bent has not been broken there. On three sides, a forest line surrounds the constructed face of the city, on the fourth a fjord reaches into the land with houses lining the shore, a mouth full of teeth.

It is here that Waitz's running becomes elemental, un-leashed. Houndlike, reckless and calloused towards pain, Waitz rips through timber paths, bounding over roots, duck-ing branches, splashing through tiny streams, all the while feral, pressing, driven by an ongoing passion, in rabid pursuit of her goals.

The daily effort was for a time pleasurable, a way to stay fit. It was intensely personal.

The Norwegian Track and Field Federation, meanwhile, decided to offer finances to help support her while she trained. Waitz refused the aid. "I wanted to run for myself and not the country. I put the training program away, didn't want to have any connection with the federation scholarship. I wanted to feel free and do what I wanted myself.

"Today I don't think about the 1976 Olympics but I think I've learned something from it. I enjoy my running more now, because I feel I have no pressure and I don't care so much if I have a bad race."

Her love of running in the woods of Oslo gave her returns, later, in 1977, when she resumed running. She began to run cross-country races. She was accustomed to the irregular surface, to the soft giving ground. In various races throughout Europe, she set the forests afire. In 1978, 1979 and 1980 she won the International Cross-Country Championships. Some say she has more talent for cross-country than for any other event, including the marathon. She has never lost a cross-country race.

In the last 7 miles of the 1978 New York Marathon, Waitz passed Martha Cooksey who was straining to run under 2:30. Waitz, beyond 20 miles, began to feel the stress of running a distance she had never attempted before. The blood in her legs seemed to thicken to mud. The finish line seemed another marathon-length away. Clamorous crowds exhorted her to break the record. She wasn't thinking of records. Not then. Pain has a way of prolonging those momentary lapses of intellect.

As she crossed the finish line, arms aloft, the announcer shouted her number only. He didn't know her name. Only then did she know of the record, only later, nursing her aching thighs, did she realize what it had taken to achieve it.

The speed with which women crossed over into the male roadrunning world, was for most people astonishing. Most men couldn't conceive of running 26.2 miles. "But a woman?" Ten years ago women were not allowed to run in any marathons. The traditional thinking was that women's bodies were too fragile to withstand the stress of running a marathon. Their ears would fall off, perhaps; their delicate legs splinter and crack. They might even go blind? No—doctors sincerely believed it would be harmful. Their breasts would sag, their reproductive systems droop and break down. But evidence by researchers and personal experiments by thousands of women runners have proven the conservative doctors wrong. They could run marathons safely and in some cases were going to finish ahead of men.

In a now-famous story, Katharine Switzer ran "officially" in the Boston Marathon. It was Patriots Day in Boston, 1967. She signed up as K.V. Switzer, with marathon officials unaware that "K.V." were the initials of a woman. When the press noticed her behind a hooded sweatshirt, race director Will Cloney was told. Without jogging shorts, without sneakers (and that is what they were still called then) the fired-up Cloney ran after her. She was too fast for him. Then co-director Jack Simple was after her attempting, officially of course, to rip her number off. Switzer's boyfriend, rather large as runners go, drove Simple into the curb and off the roadway. Switzer, running unmolested for the remainder of the race, finished in 4:30.

Then the real controversy began. Women were sneaking from behind bushes and into races all over the United States. The running establishment was confused. Doctors began to change their opinions on women's physical weaknesses. And the feminist movement fired women runners to continue to push for official status.

In 1972 women were given recognition. Nina Kuscik, in her thirties, mother of three, was the first woman finisher in the first Boston Marathon officially open to women.

Now there are races exclusively for women. There are an estimated 6.5 million women joggers in the United States. Race times are shortening in bounds. Women are beginning to train the same distances and as hard as men.

Grete Waitz has been exemplary in this regard. She has withstood rigorous training for ten years and says it is the reason her results have surpassed those of American female runners. Patti Lyons, a top woman runner from Boston, put it this way: "She's making girls realize that they can't work out like girls. They have to work out like athletes."

Early predictions saw women free from the "suffocation of sexist roles" and potentially running abreast of men. That hasn't happened and probably won't. Researchers have found that women are not as strong as men. They have proportionately smaller hearts and more body fat. Yet they have found, too, that in sweating, endurance and efficiency in body movement, women are equal to men.

But the point is not, as some have said, to compare women to a masculine standard. Women runners are saying they are learning "to listen to their own bodies," "to achieve their own potential." Yet, it is true, however, that women still have not received equal opportunities in the marathon. The longest event for women in the Olympics is 1,500 meters. The

International Olympic Committee is still afraid, one thinks, that the distance is too long for women, still worrying about women's ears falling off.

For Grete Waitz the situation is frustrating. The shorter distances are more difficult for her. Longer events in the Olympics would be a new goal—something the training-weary Grete Waitz is looking for. Although she's not concerned with honors, longer events would almost surely secure a gold medal for Waitz and the world recognition she deserves.

"I don't think it is fair," she says, "that women are not allowed to run longer than 1,500 meters in the Olympics. In all other competitions they have proven that they can run long-distance events. And all over the world a lot of women are training for longer distances, but they can't run in the Olympics. I hope that in 1984 they will have an event for long-distance runners also."

If more proof is needed for the International Olympic Committee to allow longer women's events in the Olympics, they might check in the newspapers under New York City Marathon, October 23, 1979. Look for the name Grete Waitz.

I looked for her. I was standing in a sweating crowd, squinting out over a black-top drive in Central Park that seemed to swell and roll in the heat. It was a 74-degree Indian summer day. My shirt stuck to my back. My eyes were weary from watching runners pass. There is a mesmerism in watching a race—the constant stream of runners, the riotous, intricate sound of crowd approval. Unless you close your eyes, they will follow the runners inadvertently, much in the same way that people's eyes in a bar will always keep returning to a bright television set. After a while it's dizzying, and bodies begin to run together like colors and your eyes sting as if clouded with smoke. I wondered, feeling wretched standing in the heat, how the runners felt after running the length of this wholesome but still crazed race.

I eventually could make out the lined, dogged figure of Grete Waitz. She was up on a small wave on the rolling street, up on a cloud of haze and smog, and in New York City, who knows what else. She was as poised as always, her muscles swelled and sharp, her running lyric and light. Each of her strides reflecting the other. Her arms steadying her. Her graceful movements repeating themselves with the rhythm of wings.

At the halfway point Waitz was running 4 seconds faster than last year. Except for some stomach cramps earlier, she ran without mishap. Over the Queensboro Bridge her husband told her she was on a record pace. "I complained as I usually do when I see him," she said. "I said 'My legs are stiff and sore.' But he knows me and he knows I'm always complaining." The second-place finisher, Gillian Adams, who came in 10 minutes behind Waitz, complained too. "The last time I saw her (Waitz), she was at the starting gate . . ."

Into Central Park, fiery fall leaves whirred as she passed them. Her lead was clear. There were men in front of her, men behind. They were running near 5:30 per mile and a woman was right beside them. Waitz paced herself on the strides of a man whose speed she thought she could maintain. To the exultant crowd the male bodies were simple fillers in a dramatic display of feminine power. Their clanging support didn't let up. In a few adrenaline-pulsed miles, Grete Waitz, a woman, would finish a marathon in a time that any man twenty years earlier would consider a ridiculous possibility. If for some unforeseen reason Waitz crippled in those last miles, the crowd on its toes, swaying in its density, would probably have carried Waitz on its communal shoulders across the finish line.

A *New York Times* editorial said of Grete Waitz's new world record: "There may be more important indices of women's progress in recent years but probably none so dramatic as 2 hours 27 minutes 33 seconds." Her time gave overwhelming testimony that women could run marathons as safely and as well as men.

Waitz, however, hadn't looked at it that way. "If my time in the New York City Marathon has helped the cause of longer women's events in the Olympics I think that is a good thing. But I must say I don't think so much upon it and I don't feel proud. For me it was a race just like other races. I very seldom think back on races. I look forward to new challenges. But of course I was happy and very pleased with my time in the New York City Marathon."

Unlike some of the more overzealous running proponents who have offered running to cure the common cold, give us back religion, reunite the atom and provide for a daily personal panacea, running is running to Grete Waitz. It is fun. It is sport. Placing it outside these two categories draws her outspoken criticism. She doesn't understand running American-style, although her recent exposure has made it more comprehensible. She doesn't understand how women could take drugs to improve their performances. (Seven women athletes were banned from running last year because of their use of anabolic steroids to improve their performances.) "Steroids have nothing to do with sport and for me it took something away from running, because it is hard to push yourself in training twice a day when you know that some of your competitors are using artificial things to run faster. I can't understand that some women are willing to do such a dangerous thing with their body only to run faster. It is important to inform young people about how dangerous the use of steroids is. If they use steroids their body can be destroyed for the rest of their life and it isn't worth that. Not even an Olympic gold medal."

And politics seems to contain a similar poison for sport. "It is a bad thing that they shall put sport and politics together but it has always been so. I think it is not so easy to separate them as long as a lot of countries use sport as a part of their political system. Something I don't like is that people are using sport as a political weapon, because it is the most easy and convenient thing to do. For example using sport as a political weapon instead of using other sanctions, like economical."

If you ask Waitz about the future her answers are more noncommital. How fast do you think you could run a marathon? She doesn't know. "I'm a track runner. I don't train for the marathon. I'm not patient enough to train for the marathon. To run more than an hour at a time is boring." How well do you think women will do the marathon? She shakes her head. Can't predict. How about the Olympics? Unsure. And having a baby? No time now. Maybe later. Finally what are her running plans for the future? She shifts uncomfortably, her speech lurches—I've put her up against the wall. "It's harder and harder to train hard and push myself. I've been in two Olympics. I've been training internationally for ten years. Five years ago I was really motivated. My goal now is to win the World Championships in Paris in March (she placed first). What is happening after that, I don't know . . .

Recently women's marathons have been added to both

the 1982 European Championships in Athens and the first world track championships in Helsinki in 1983. Prospects are good for a women's marathon in the 1984 Olympics in Los Angeles. Hans Skasit, president of the Norwegian Amateur Athletic Federation told *Runners World*, "Grete Waitz has done the marathon in a way every man must accept. She has done it the man's way. They have to shut up about a 2:25. There is nothing more to say."

Predictions are being made on how fast women will soon run the marathon. Some say, by the end of the decade, women will run 2:18. David C. Costell, Ph.D., in an article in *The Runner* magazine, thinks that Grete Waitz has the speed to run much faster probably below 2:25. Fred Lebow says that with training she will be the first women to run 2:22.

Waitz even when pressed refuses to predict what women will do. As for her own time? Bill Rodgers, the American male record holder in the marathon told me that it sometimes takes him three weeks to recover from a difficult marathon. After her first marathon Waitz could barely walk and had to have treatments to relieve her aching thighs. After the 1979 New York City Marathon there was no ache. She ran 10 kilometers the next day. The following day, she ran twice. "I recovered overnight I think," she said.

Grete Waitz continues to break her own records. Her best time in the marathon so far is 2:25:41. That time is on tenuous ground for the 1981 N.Y.C. Marathon. She has shown throughout her career that she is the greatest woman distance runner that has ever lived. She has also shown that she wishes she could run from all the attention this honor brings. She doesn't want to be famous, she's said. "I don't want to be a runner twenty-four hours a day. I want to be a normal person." It would be good for Grete Waitz, she makes you think, if she could run alone, unfettered and unknown through the woods of Oslo with numbers of trees watching silently. But what a pity, I thought, if no one was given the chance to see her run.

R.M.

Index

Index

ABOUT THE AUTHORS

THOMAS BARRETT lives in Rye, New York. He is a lawyer, father of five children, and a runner. He has run many races from the mile to 62 miles, including many marathons.

ROBERT MORRISSEY, JR., lives and works in Mamaroneck, New York. He graduated from Boston College and attended Boston University's Graduate School of Public Communications. He writes mostly about the outdoors. This is his first book.

920
BAR

Barrett, Thomas

Marathon runners

DATE			